James Joyce's Dublin Houses

& *Nora Barnacle's Galway*

D1340564

VIVIEN IGOE is a graduate of University College Dublin. She worked as Curator of the James Joyce Museum in Sandycove, County Dublin, from 1965 to 1972. She is an authority and a lecturer on Joyce and in 1967 organized the First International James Joyce Symposium, which was held in Dublin. She was chairman of the James Joyce Institute of Ireland from 1980 to 1985.

By the same author:

A Literary Guide to Dublin
City of Dublin
Dublin Burial Grounds & Graveyards

James Joyce's
Dublin Houses

& Nora Barnacle's Galway

VIVIEN IGOE

THE LILLIPUT PRESS • DUBLIN

First published 2007 by
THE LILLIPUT PRESS LTD
62–63 Sitric Road, Arbour Hill, Dublin 7, Ireland
www.lilliputpress.ie

A CIP record for this title is available from the British Library.

ISBN 978 1 84351 082 6

Set in 11 on 15 point Bulmer
Book Design and Typesetting by Anú Design, Tara
Printed in England by Cromwell Press, Wiltshire

For Michael

Contents

Acknowledgments

I would like to thank my dear mother, Eileen Veale, who gave me an interest in James Joyce in the first instance.

My very special thanks are due to Paddy Tutty and Brian Lynch, in the Photographic Department, Bord Fáilte, for their assistance; also to the staff in the National Library of Ireland for their unfailing courtesy.

Thanks are due to Father Fergus O'Donoghue, SJ, and Malachy and Eamon O'Brien, for some hitherto-unpublished photographs of great Joycean interest.

For some points of information I would like to thank the following: Mary Clark, Phil Coleman, Paddy Donnelly, Neil Harpur, Liz McManus, Michael C. Moloney, Ken Monaghan, Robert Nicholson, John C. Ryan, Paul Stephenson, Patrick Shine of Dublin City Council, and my brothers Thomas and Michael Veale. Thanks also to Ann Igoe for her cheerful company walking the routes.

In Galway, I would like to thank Maeve Doyle and Joe O'Halloran, from University College; and a very special thanks to Sheila and Mary Gallagher from the Nora Barnacle House, Bowling Green.

For permission to quote extracts from the works of James Joyce, I am grateful to the executors of the Estate of James Joyce and the Society of Authors, as the literary representatives of the Estate of James Joyce.

List of Illustrations

Photographs on pages 4, 7, 18 (top), 20, 23, 27, 36, 45, 75, 106 (top), 109 and 120 are from the Lawrence Collection and are reproduced courtesy of the National Library of Ireland; page 26 is reproduced courtesy of Malachy O'Brien; page 30 is reproduced courtesy of Ken Monaghan; page 51 is reproduced courtesy of Fr Fergus O'Donoghue, SJ; pages 91 and 121 are reproduced courtesy of Mrs G. Solterer; page 104 is reproduced courtesy of Sheila Gallagher. Rose Cottage (page 2) is reproduced courtesy of *The Cork Examiner* and Phil Coleman.

The maps were prepared by Maria Killeen.

Based on Ordnance Survey Ireland Permit No. 8120.
Copyright Ordnance Survey Ireland and Government of Ireland.

A NOTE ON THE MAPS
The maps relate only to the areas where Joyce lived. For more detailed information on streets and roads, the reader may find it helpful to consult the Ordnance Survey Street Map of Dublin.

Preface

The purpose of this book is to describe in detail the many houses in Dublin where the Joyce family lived. The constant moving caused great disruption and hardship but, on the positive side, Joyce gained an intimate knowledge of the city. The importance of it is that he wrote his books; the significance of the houses he lived in is the artistic use to which he put them in his works.

When John Stanislaus Joyce, the father of James Joyce, came to Dublin from Cork in 1874, he was a wealthy man, having inherited eleven properties; added to this was a thousand pounds, which he received on his twenty-first birthday. Shortly after his marriage to Mary Jane Murray in 1880, he secured a well-paid job in the Office of the Collector of Rates in Dublin, leaving him very comfortably off. Described as a bon vivant, he was gregarious, volatile, and a heavy drinker. He was incapable of managing his money and in a short time had squandered his fortune. The result was that his family led a semi-nomadic existence, drifting from house to house; in the later years, these moves were to the poorer and sometimes central areas of the city.

John Joyce changed address eighteen times between 1880 and the time of Joyce's final departure from Dublin. Luckily, moving was made comparatively easy for him and his family as Dublin was in the doldrums regarding its development as a city; rents were low and there was a lot of property available to let.

Joyce had a few more Dublin addresses; added to the family homes were his furnished room in Shelbourne Road, his stays with James H. Cousins in Dromard Terrace, Sandymount, and the Murrays in North Strand Road, his days in the Martello Tower and his return visits to Dublin, when he stayed at 44 Fontenoy Street, and again when he paid his final visit in 1912 when he stayed at both 17 and 21 Richmond Place, North Circular Road.

The reasons for John Joyce's moves were varied. His first move from Kingstown to Brighton Square was to escape unpleasant memories of the death of his son. The expansion of the family prompted the move from Brighton Square to Castlewood Avenue, and from here he moved to Bray to escape from his wife's relations. It was also a fashionable area at the time; it was at this address that John Joyce lost his job which made him move to Carysfort Avenue in Blackrock.

The move from here to the city, and subsequent moves, resulted from John Joyce's unwillingness to pay the rent. He could not manage to drink as much as he did and pay the rent at the same time. Carysfort Avenue was the last of their suburban residences on the south side. Once they crossed the river from the south side, they never recrossed it again as a family. The north side was significant even then as being the less fashionable side of the city. In general, the Joyces moved quite a distance from one house to another. However, Fairview on the north side was the exception. Here they had four addresses in close proximity; Windsor Avenue, Convent Avenue, Richmond Avenue and Royal Terrace. To delay the disruption of evictions, John Joyce resorted to various tricks. One of these was to negotiate with the landlord to give him a receipt for the rent on the understanding that he would leave the premises, saving the landlord any legal costs. To get rid of a bad tenant like John Joyce, the landlord would oblige and issue him with receipts for a few months' unpaid rent. This receipt acted as a reference, enabling him to get other accommodation, generally a smaller house in a poorer area. In Convent Avenue, while house-sharing, John Joyce and the other tenant exchanged rent receipts, as though each had been the other's landlord. Joyce's new landlord in Richmond Avenue was unaware that he had been evicted from his former house.

Before the death of his wife, John Joyce commuted half of his pension to buy a house in St Peter's Terrace. This was the only house he ever owned in Dublin. It is interesting to note that even by today's standards, all the houses that he occupied have kept their relative values. Of all the houses inhabited by Joyce in Dublin, all but two of them (the demolished Georgian house in Hardwicke Street and 2 Millbourne Avenue) may be seen today.

When Joyce left Ireland with Nora Barnacle, he continued the pattern set in his early years, of drifting from place to place, never settling anywhere for very long. Like his father, he was restless, continually changing his abode, sometimes through circumstances, no doubt, but also on account of his nature. His early moves on the continent to Pola, Trieste, Rome and back to Trieste, concerned his jobs, which consisted of teaching and a job in a bank. There were numerous moves within each of the places that Joyce settled in, including accommodation in rooms, guesthouses, hotels and apartments.

His next move, in 1915 to Zurich, was due to the outbreak of the First World War. In 1920 he went to live in Paris in order to get his work published and to gain international recognition. The reason for his return to Zurich in 1940 was the outbreak of the Second World War. Despite Nora's wishes to remain in one location, Joyce's early experience left him unable to settle anywhere.

Introduction

After the Act of Union in 1800, the momentum of Dublin's expansion faltered and by 1900 the city was almost a hundred years behind the times. It was undoubtedly still a capital city but a second-rate one. The excesses of Victorian architecture had made little impression on the streetscape and the original Georgian splendour was still in evidence, even if it did suffer from almost a century of neglect. Never having been an industrial city, Dublin lacked an inner dynamism for expansion and the census returns show only a modest rise in the population of five per cent in the last decade of the nineteenth century.

The fall of Parnell in 1890 had a traumatic effect on the psyche of the Irish nation. He had Home Rule almost within his grasp when he was named as co-respondent by Captain William O'Shea in his divorce action against his wife, Kathleen. The divorce was granted and the non-conformist element in Gladstone's party was outraged, demanding that Parnell be removed as leader of the Irish Party. Parnell refused to yield and the party split. He died suddenly in October 1891 and for the next ten years Ireland was politically powerless and without a leader.

John Stanislaus Joyce had been a passionate supporter of Parnell and saw in his fall a mirror image of the Joyce family fortunes. To the end of his life John Joyce remained a Parnellite, railing against false friends and betrayers. His son, James, shared his political opinions and summed up what he saw as the Irish attitude to Parnell by saying, 'They did not throw him to the wolves, they tore him to pieces themselves.'

At the turn of the century Dublin was a Roman Catholic city, but one in which the Protestant minority, which represented about twenty per cent of the population, held most of the mercantile, professional and executive power and wealth. The flight of the middle classes to the suburbs, which started in the 1830s with the building of the Dublin to Kingstown railway, and gained momentum with the introduction of the tramway network, continued into the early 1900s.

Within the city there was a great deal of dire poverty and unemployment, but virtually all businesses were still located within the boundaries of the Grand and Royal Canals. Many of the old, fashionable, residential districts on the north side of the city had been bought by speculative landlords who let out the houses, in flats or rooms, to artisans and working-class families. Gradually, these houses fell into disrepair and degenerated into slums.

Areas south of the Liffey fared better. Many houses here were bought by members of the legal and medical professions, when the seal of approval of social and professional success was a baronetcy or knighthood. In the early years of this century there were so many titled medical men in the city that Dublin was known as the 'City of Dreadful Knights'. In this way, the areas around Merrion and Fitzwilliam Squares held both their status and their value.

Some Dubliners still had some pretensions to grandeur; for instance, it was claimed that the best English was spoken in Dublin and that the city was 'the seventh in Christendom'. Unfortunately, neither of these assertions could stand up to close scrutiny.

Cultural life in Dublin was rather limited. In 1900 it had five theatres, two of which were music halls. The most popular theatrical events of the year were the pantomimes. The Gaiety and the Royal theatres played a large part in the social life of the city and relied heavily on London companies, such as the D'Oyly Carte and the Carl Rosa Opera, for drama, musical comedies and light operas. The Queen's Theatre provided a staple diet of melodrama and sentimental patriotic plays, such as *The Face in the Window* or *Arrah na Pogue*, but by far the most popular venues for ordinary Dubliners were the Empire Palace and Tivoli. These music halls offered variety shows, which were often cheap and vulgar but always entertaining. The Abbey Theatre, which was founded in 1904 as a literary theatre, appealed only to a minority and, because of this, it often played to very poor houses. Joyce was scornful of this theatrical effort and accused them of producing only 'dwarf drama'.

The musical life of the city was even more limited and elitist. On the occasions when there were celebrity concerts, they were given on weekday afternoons, which ensured that the vast majority of the population could not attend. The opera seasons always included such old reliables as *The Bohemian Girl*, *The Lily of Killarney*, *Martha* and *Carmen*. Lovers of Grand Opera were poorly catered for. Ordinary Dubliners appreciated the concerts given by Irish artists in the Rotunda and the Antient Concert Rooms, where, in 1904 James Joyce shared the platform with John McCormack.

The foundation of the Gaelic Athletic Association and Gaelic League in the late nineteenth century reawakened a realization of Irish traditions and culture across the sectarian divide in Ireland. For a number of years after the death of Parnell, Ireland was in the political doldrums. However, never far beneath the surface of Irish life was the movement for complete political independence from Britain. In 1898 the Irish Republican Brotherhood recovered support when it took a leading role in the celebrations to commemorate the centenary of the Rising of 1798. It was the Military Council of the IRB which planned the Rising of 1916.

However, in the Dublin of 1900, few people appreciated the political or literary forces that were at work in the city and which were to come to fruition more than twenty years later when, in 1922, the Irish Free State was established and in Paris, *Ulysses* was published by Shakespeare & Co.

I
Birth to Bray,
1882–91

Rose Cottage, now known as Grange Cottage, was the birthplace of James Augustine Joyce, the grandfather of James Joyce. Built in 1750, the cottage is located in the Grange area of Fermoy in a laneway known as Joyce's Boreen, which leads to the River Blackwater. (Approach Fermoy Bridge from the Dublin side and take the Mallow Road. At first crossroads, turn left and the second house on the right-hand side nearest the river is Rose Cottage.)

JAMES JOYCE'S great-grandfather, George Joyce, was a man of property in Cork. His grandfather, James Augustine Joyce, after whom the author was named, was born in 1827, at Rose Cottage in Fermoy, County Cork. In 1848 he married Ellen O'Connell who came from a prosperous family in the Iveragh peninsula in County Kerry. She was related to the great Daniel O'Connell, the Liberator, and two of her cousins, John Daly MP and Peter Paul McSwiney, were Lord Mayors of Cork and Dublin, respectively. It is interesting to note that in *Ulysses*, Simon Dedalus claims relationship with McSwiney.

James Augustine Joyce and Ellen O'Connell had only one child, a son named John Stanislaus, who was born on 4 July 1849. He attended St Colman's College in Fermoy, where in 1859 he was the youngest pupil and was given special tuition in piano and singing.

Being the only child of prosperous parents there was an easygoing attitude taken to the school work and to his behaviour. In an interview published in the *James Joyce Yearbook*, in 1949, which John Joyce had given before his death in 1931, he spoke of his connection with Daniel O'Connell. He often heard his mother say that when O'Connell drove his carriage from Derrynane to Cork City, he would pull up at her

St Colman's College, Fermoy, which John Stanislaus Joyce attended in 1859.

Queen's College, Cork, where John Joyce studied medicine.

father's shop in Great George's Street. Then, wearing their knee breeches, her father and the Liberator would walk arm in arm down the street. His mother told him that O'Connell would often do the round trip in his carriage from Kerry to Cork and back in one day.

In the same interview, John Joyce gave a description of his youth in Cork:

'Every night of my life and in the daytime too, I think of all these things – they all come back to me and, my God, when I think of the times I used to have and here I am now – well, I had a good time anyway. There is not a field in County Cork that I don't know, for I hunted them all and now I go through all these hunts and jollifications that we used to have after them. They were great. I was one of the best men after the harriers. We had a great pack and I was one of the best on foot. When at College – the Queen's in Cork – I took several exhibitions but I lost the certificates long ago. I put my portmanteau in pawn one time for ten shillings with a pawnbroker named Cunningham, in Marlborough Street. He was a decent fellow. There was a set of false teeth and certificates which were in it.'

However, the College has no record of having granted any certificates to John Stanislaus Joyce.

On his twenty-first birthday, John Joyce inherited properties in Cork, which brought him a yearly income of three hundred pounds. His grandfather, John O'Connell, also gave him one thousand pounds. Not being successful at his medical studies, he decided to join the French army at the outbreak of the Franco-Prussian War but was intercepted by his mother *en route* in London. In 1874 she moved from Cork to Dublin, thinking that this might have better prospects for the talents of her son, then aged twenty-five.

For his part, John Joyce was in no particular hurry to seek employment as he was comfortably off. He enjoyed sailing and with his fine tenor voice, sang in the occasional concert and soiree.

In 1877 John Joyce met Henry Alleyne, another flamboyant Corkonian and a friend of his late father. He was manager and Chairman of the Dublin and Chapelizod Distillery Company. George Delaney, yet another Cork man, was a Director, as was John Dunbar, afterwards MP for New Ross and a brother-in-law of Alleyne.

The distillery, which was situated in the picturesque village of Chapelizod three miles west of Dublin city centre, was established in 1878. There was a steam tramway which passed the premises, giving easy access to Dublin. Prior to being a whiskey distillery, the building had been a military barracks, a convent, and a fulling mill and flax factory, which was set up by William Dargan, the Irish railway entrepreneur. Being such a large and extensive building, it was easily converted into a distillery and was fitted out with the most up-to-date equipment. As there was no steam power on the premises, all the motive energy required was supplied by the Liffey, by means of a waterwheel, which stretched right across the river. It measured seventy feet in breadth and eighteen feet in diameter and was said to have been the largest in the United Kingdom. The water that was used for distilling purposes was brought from the upper reaches of the river through a closed pipe. It was a beautiful, clear stream, unlike the water at the lower reaches of the river in Dublin City.

Chapelizod has always been a favourite residential area for discerning Dubliners. It derived its name from 'chapel of Isolde', which is said to date back to Arthurian times when La belle Iseult lived in the area. It was noted for its remarkable scenery, especially along the banks of the Liffey towards Lucan, where there were extensive strawberry beds spread over two miles on the northern slope of the vale.

Henry Alleyne must have cut a bit of a dash in his day as each morning he drove out from his home in Dublin in his carriage, which

Chapelizod, County Dublin. The distillery is far left and adjoining it is the house where John Joyce lived.

was drawn by a fine, high-stepping, bay horse that was harnessed with patent-leather and silver fittings. To add to the colour a servant, attired in livery with his arms folded, sat behind him!

Alleyne invited John Joyce to invest five hundred pounds in the distillery. Joyce agreed, provided that he was made Secretary of the company at three hundred pounds a year, which was an excellent salary in 1877. The Directors agreed and John Joyce commenced work at his first job in Dublin. At the time, there was a steady demand for this particular whiskey, which was supplied to wholesalers and retailers direct from the spirit store. Known as 'Dublin Whiskey', it had a high reputation with its mellow flavour and characteristic bouquet. The annual output was 350,000 gallons, which found a market chiefly in London and the Colonies. Sixty persons were employed in the distillery and seven Excise Officers.

Although Alleyne was not popular with the distillery staff, John Joyce got on well with him and was astounded when he detected irregularities in the accounts. He discovered that Alleyne had embezzled considerable sums from the company and this resulted in its closure. Its name was subsequently changed to Phoenix Park Distillery when it was bought by the Distillers Company Ltd. It eventually closed in 1920 and nothing of it remains today except an outer wall.

When the fraud was discovered, Alleyne disappeared without trace and was never heard of again. John Joyce, although he received the thanks of the Directors for discovering the fraud, lost his five hundred pounds and his job. Later, his son James, who enjoyed paying off his father's old scores, included Mr Alleyne as a disagreeable employer in 'Counterparts', one of the stories in *Dubliners*.

John Joyce was always 'talking of feints and worms', which were used in the distilling process and had 'endless stories about the distillery' like old Cotter in 'The Sisters'. Joyce refers to his father's connection with Chapelizod in most of his works; in *Finnegans Wake*, it is termed 'the still that was the mill'; in 'A Painful Case' Mr Duffy, the saturnine bachelor, chose to reside in Chapelizod, 'because he found all the other suburbs of Dublin mean, modern and pretentious'. He lived in a sombre old house with a view of the river which 'lay quiet beside the distillery'. Joyce chose for Mr Duffy the house that had once been the home of his father. This house, which was situated opposite the churchyard, was demolished in 1978.

In later years, amongst the books in John Joyce's library, there was a copy of J. Sheridan Le Fanu's book *The House by the Churchyard*. Le Fanu used the Chapelizod of 1767 as the setting for his novel. Many of the eighteenth-century landmarks still remain there today, including the actual house by the churchyard beside the Protestant Church, just south of Anna Livia Bridge.

The house is referred to in many different forms in *Finnegans Wake* such as the 'old house for the chargehard'; 'the old house by the churpelizod'; 'De oud huis bjj de kerkegaard'; 'In the church by the hearseyard', and so on. Humphrey Chimpden Earwicker, the hero of

Finnegans Wake, lived in Chapelizod with his family where he was the publican in The Mullingar House. A plaque on this building commemorates the Joycean connection.

John Joyce spent three or four years working as Secretary for the distillery and remarked that he used to have great times then. He lived

The House by the Churchyard in Chapelizod, which is referred to in Finnegans Wake.

in the town, had friends such as the Broadbent family who owned the Mullingar Hotel (now Mullingar House), and he partook in local jollifications. He was an excellent sportsman and won a prize as champion bowler in a match between the Distillery and the Dollymount Clubs.

'We beat Dollymount and I made a big score; and, by God, I was carried around the place and such a time we had. I beat my man to love – anyway I gave him a good beating. I was made a lot of and was taken around by the boys on their shoulders; and, my God, the quantity of whiskey that I drank that night! It must have been something terrible for I had to go to bed. I was not very long in bed when half a dozen of the fellows came up to me and said that they were having a singsong downstairs, adding: "Come on Jack, don't have them beat us at the singing."'

Sometime later in the interview published in 1949, when asked if he knew anything about the quality of the water of the Liffey, he replied, 'Not a damn bit, because I never drank it without whiskey in it.'

John Murray of Longford, an agent for wines and spirits, was a customer at the distillery. John Joyce used to visit him at his home in Upper Clanbrassil Street and it was here that he met Murray's only daughter, the nineteen-year-old Mary Jane, who was known as 'May'. She was pretty, fair-haired, intelligent and had a talent for music, having studied the piano and had her voice trained from the age of five, at the Misses Flynn School, at 15 Usher's Island on the Dublin quays. The school was run by two of her mother's sisters, Mrs Callanan and Mrs Lyons, both of whom appear under the guise of the Misses Morkan in Joyce's story 'The Dead'.

The young couple shared an interest in music and sang together on Sundays in the choir of the Church of the Three Patrons in Rathgar. This was one of the best church choirs in Dublin in the

The Church of Our Lady of Refuge, Rathmines, where John Joyce and Mary Jane Murray were married on 5 May 1880.

1880s. John Murray, known as 'Red Murray', did not wish his daughter to continue her friendship with John Joyce, knowing that he was a heavy drinker and also that he had broken off two previous engagements in fits of jealousy. Murray forbade the match, a fact that John Joyce remembered all his life. John Joyce's mother was not in favour of it either.

One day in Grafton Street, John Murray met his daughter in the company of John Joyce and became very angry. He made a scene and ordered a cab to take his daughter home. A worried onlooker asked John Joyce what was the matter, and he replied, 'Oh, nothing serious. Just the usual story of a beautiful daughter and the irascible parent.' Murray appears in *Ulysses* and also provided material for *Dubliners*.

John Joyce never forgot even minor affronts to his pride. He had no love for the Murray family, with the exception of May's mother who approved of him marrying her daughter. He was quite persistent, even to the point of moving to the same street as his fiancée. The address given on his marriage certificate was 14 Clanbrassil Street, while that of the Murrays was number seven. Interestingly, in *Ulysses*, the fictional Rudolph Bloom, born Rudolph Virag, lived in 52 Clanbrassil Street, after his marriage to Ellen Higgins in August 1865. A plaque marks the house, as their son, the equally fictional Leopold Bloom, was said to have been born there in May 1866.

John Joyce and May Murray were married on 5 May 1880 in the Church of Our Lady of Refuge, Rathmines, when May was twenty, and her husband ten years older. About this time, John Joyce's mother returned from the house she had rented in Dalkey, Country Dublin, to Cork. She died shortly afterwards without forgiving her son. Joyce was to incorporate the same traits of pride in 'The Dead', when Gabriel Conroy's mother opposes his marriage.

They chose London for their honeymoon and on their return lived for very brief periods at 13 Ontario Terrace, Rathmines and 30 Emorville Avenue, off the South Circular Road, before moving to a large Victorian house at 47 Northumberland Avenue, Kingstown (now Dun Laoghaire). Situated off Upper George's Street, and opposite the Methodist Church, this was a large end-of-terrace Victorian house, two-storeys over a basement, with a further extension at the back and a very long garden. Due to reconstruction, only the façade remains unchanged. John Joyce was still financially very comfortable, and shortly after his marriage secured a permanent job in the Office of the Collector of Rates in Dublin, which was located at 43 Fleet Street, in the city centre. In addition to his income from his investments, he now had a salary of five hundred pounds a year. This should have had a stabilising effect on him, since up to this time he had been unsuccessful in all of his chosen occupations. Stephen Dedalus summed up his father's career in *A Portrait of the Artist as a Young Man* as that of 'a medical student, an oarsman, a tenor, an amateur actor, a shouting politician, a small landlord, a small investor, a drinker, a good fellow, a story-teller, somebody's secretary, something in a distillery, a tax-gatherer, and, at present, a praiser of his own past.'

John Joyce's first child, a son who survived only a fortnight, was born in 1881. Shortly afterwards May became pregnant again and John

41 Brighton Square, James Joyce's birthplace.

Joyce took out the first mortgage on his Cork properties. Even at this early stage, the pattern of his financial downfall was beginning to emerge. Between the years 1881 and 1894, he contracted mortgages on his eleven Cork properties and fathered thirteen children, ten of whom survived. It was probably the association of the death of their first baby and the unpleasant memories it had that prompted the Joyces to move to 41 Brighton Square, Rathgar, a quiet middle-class suburb in Dublin. Here, their neighbours were professional people including a barrister, a solicitor, an accountant, a bank manager and a district surveyor with the Board of Works.

Rathgar is situated three miles from the city centre. The whole area was open fields until the 1860s, when the first development was the construction of the 'New Road', now Rathgar Road, while an old field path became Rathgar Avenue. In the 1880s, the Rathmines Township, which included Rathgar, had a population of nearly twenty-five thousand and was described as being one of the most pleasing outlets of the metropolis, studded with handsome terraces and detached villas, and several pretty avenues diverging from the centre and leading towards Harold's Cross, the River Dodder, Terenure and Upper Rathmines. Conveniently, there was a tramway from Dublin to Terenure, which was a short walk from the Joyce home.

John Joyce was restless by nature and did not wish to tie himself down by buying a house and so always chose to rent one. Many people at that time rented accommodation of which there was no shortage on the market. When the Joyces lived in Rathgar, out of the seventy-seven houses on Brighton Square, nine were vacant.

In 1881, 41 Brighton Square, built in five years earlier, had had only one previous occupant, a Colonel Richard Harbord. It was in this modest, redbrick, Victorian terraced house that James Augustine Joyce, named after his paternal grandfather, was born on 2 February 1882. The house, with a two-storey front and a three-storey back, is much larger than its exterior would indicate. The ground floor comprises a hallway with an ornate ceiling. Located off this is the drawing-room, which has an embossed brass bay window, and the dining-room, which has a later addition of French doors that lead to a glazed conservatory. Both rooms have decorative friezes and white marble fireplaces and are separated by interconnecting doors. An interesting feature in the hallway is the brass rail attached to the wall, which was used by gentlemen to hold while their muddied boots were being removed. At the end of the hallway, four steps lead down to a very comfortable kitchen and scullery area. There is a large storeroom, and a coal-store. On the first floor, spanning the width of the house and incorporating the two front windows, is the large master bedroom, which is probably the room Joyce was born in. There are three other bedrooms, two with fireplaces, and a bathroom. There is a neat, well-kept, walled garden to the rear with a garage and entrance from a laneway.

Joyce's birthplace started him off on a bizarre note. Brighton Square is not a square but a triangle, comprising one acre, two roads and two perches. The house is marked by a bronze plaque that reads:

> *Birthplace of James Joyce, Poet and Novelist,*
> *1882–1941.*
> *Presented by Montclair State College, New Jersey.*
> *Bloomsday, 1964.*

This was the beginning of the Odyssean peregrination, which ended on a cold January day in 1941 in Fluntern cemetery, Zurich.

James Joyce was baptized in the small chapel-of-ease at Roundtown on 5 February 1882 by the curate, the Reverend Father John O'Mulloy. The Reverend John Deasy was the other curate in the parish. This was the only chapel in Roundtown (later called Terenure) until the present St Joseph's Church was dedicated in 1904, near the site that was originally dedicated by Cardinal Paul Cullen in 1886.

The first written acknowledgment of Joyce is the simple entry number 896, written by the parish clerk, in the church records. The clerk made an error in writing the middle name as 'Augusta' instead of Augustine. Joyce's godparents were a ship's chandler called Philip McCann and his wife Ellen (née Callanan), who was his great-aunt. Philip McCann appears in Joyce's last work, *Finnegans Wake*, while

The birth registration of James Joyce in the parish records.

Ellen McCann also contributed to the character of Aunt Kate in 'The Dead'. McCann, Verdon & Co., ships chandlers, existed until 1993 at 2 Burgh Quay in Dublin, a 'marine-dealer's shop beyond the Liffey'.

Living there in his infancy, Joyce had no recollection of 41 Brighton Square; however, he includes it in *Ulysses* as one of the homes of Molly Bloom before her marriage. In the course of her final soliloquy, Molly remembers how when Bloom was courting her, he came to her house in Brighton Square and ran 'into my bedroom pretending the ink got on his hands to wash it off...O I laughed myself sick at him that day.' One night in the kitchen in Brighton Square, Bloom almost proposed. But Molly was pretending to be in a bad temper with the flour on her hands from the potato cakes she was making.

In a letter written in 1931 to his son James, John Joyce wonders if he recollected the old days in Brighton Square, 'when you were baby Tuckoo, and I used to take you out into the Square and tell you about the moo-cow that used to come down from the mountain and take little boys across'. This letter echoes the first couple of sentences in *A Portrait of the Artist as a Young Man*.

Lower Rathmines Road. Castlewood Avenue is the right turn directly behind the tram.

23 Castlewood Avenue, Rathmines.

In 1883 John Joyce took out mortgages on three of his eleven inherited Cork properties. Their first daughter, Margaret, known as 'Poppie', was born on 18 January 1884. The same year the Joyce family, now four, moved to a spacious house at 23 Castlewood Avenue, Rathmines, which extends from Lower Rathmines Road to Belgrave Square. Number twenty-three is a large double-fronted, two-storey over basement, Victorian residence consisting of five bedrooms and three reception rooms. It has a front garden and a large south-facing rear garden. It is on the corner of Cambridge Road. Rathmines, situated only two miles from the city centre, had an excellent transport service, with a tram starting every six minutes from Nelson's Pillar. It was separated from the city, at Portobello, by the Grand Canal, where the municipal and parliamentary boundaries finished. The main Rathmines Road was intersected by a number of terraces, which contained detached villas. As in their former address, this was a middle-class area and the Joyces had as neighbours an army major, an accountant, a building contractor and the animal artist, William Osborne, father of the portrait painter Walter Osborne. Their immediate neighbour was Mr Jones, Secretary of the Church of Ireland Temperance Society.

May Joyce gave birth to two children here. The next son, Stanislaus, described in *Finnegans Wake* as 'dear sweet enchainted Stainusless', was born on 17 December 1884, and Charles Patrick on 24 July 1886. They were all delivered by a midwife named Mrs Thornton of 19a Denzille Lane, whom Leopold Bloom, in *Ulysses*, is said to have summoned to deliver his daughter Milly. While living here, John Joyce found it necessary to take out a mortgage on three more of his Cork properties.

When Joyce was five and a half, he appreciated what was happening when the contents of his Castlewood Avenue home were loaded into a van and transported to another residence at 1 Martello Terrace in Bray, County Wicklow, which is thirteen miles from Dublin. This Victorian house is situated on the water's edge, at the end of a terrace of eight houses, built around 1865 by a Mr Joseph Kelly. At right angles to the seafront, it faced south along the esplanade and its northern end was adjacent to the harbour. Being so close to the sea had its disadvantages. In 1860 flooding was reported in the *Freeman's Journal* and again on 4 January 1877, it reported that 'houses at Martello Terrace, facing the esplanade, appeared as if built on an island. The water rose three or four feet in the lower storeys.' Sometime later, a small flood wall was erected directly in front of each house with steps over it. This prevented water from the high seas entering the hallways. An ornate wooden balcony was constructed at first floor level the whole length of the terrace. This, however, does not appear in the old Lawrence photograph of Martello Terrace. The original solid front door had been replaced with a door containing glass panels to let more light into the hallway, counteracting the overshadowing of the balcony.

On the ground floor there is a kitchen, as well as a dining-room and living-room that interconnect. These two rooms, both with polished marble fireplaces, have fine ceilings with frieze plasterwork of egg-and-dart design, which was fashionable at the time. The dining-room

Martello Terrace, Bray. Number 1 is the last house on the right beside the boathouse.

affording a fine, uninterrupted view of the esplanade and Bray Head, is where the Christmas dinner scene took place in *A Portrait of an Artist as a Young Man*. On the first floor return there is a small nursery or maid's room. The large drawing-room, spanning the width of the house, features a white marble fireplace and attractive ceiling cornice-work and centre rose. Tall windows open out onto the balcony. Directly behind this room is the master bedroom. On the second floor there are three bedrooms, a bathroom, and a bright landing with a partly stained glass window, affording views southwards to Killiney Bay and Dalkey. There is a walled yard at the back of the house with an outhouse that can be accessed from a rear lane. Directly in front of the terrace is a railed-in commonage, which at one time was laid out in tennis courts.

A plaque on this tastefully restored period residence reads:

James Joyce
Poet – Novelist
Lived here
1887–1891

Joyce was now in his third residence before he had reached his sixth birthday.

It was probably a combination of the lure of the sea and the wish for a larger house to accommodate his growing family that gave John Joyce the urge to move to Bray. Also, the house had the advantage of removing John Joyce farther from his wife's relations; 'the train fare would keep them away' he frequently explained.

Within easy reach of Dublin, Bray had become one of the most desirable places to live. It was termed 'the Brighton of Ireland, when Brighton was Queen of the watering places.' Scenically situated with a small population of six thousand, it had three fine hotels. Before the Joyce family moved to Bray, major improvements had been carried out on the sea front through the enterprise of William Dargan who had, in

1851, extended the Kingstown railway line to Bray. Fashionable city people took advantage of this amenity and came to take the air and walk down the fine, mile-long esplanade, also constructed by Dargan, which extended from the railway station as far as Bray Head. Carmen Sylva, the Queen of Romania, paid a visit to Bray whilst the Joyces lived there.

Joyce's brother, Stanislaus, wrote of this happy and prosperous house:

> From our windows we had a long view of the esplanade, which stretches along the seafront half the way to Bray Head, and behind it was an equally long green enclosure, and rude donkey boys. Behind there were lanes and fishermen's cottages and a long strand leading to Killiney.

The sea crashes along the wall at the side of the house and there is a wooden paling running under the first-floor windows, where Stephen Dedalus, in *A Portrait of the Artist as a Young Man*, 'saw the sea of waves, long dark waves rising and falling under the moonless night'.

It was in this healthy and fashionable district that John Joyce entertained many of his friends who travelled there by rail each Sunday. They stayed for lunch, walked down the esplanade and returned to Martello Terrace for dinner. In the dining-room on the first floor, May Joyce played the piano, while her husband and his guests sang the night away. 'We used to have merry evenings in our house, used we not?' Joyce wrote to a friend in 1934. It was probably at these musical evenings that he heard Moore's Melodies and many of the other songs that are woven through his works.

As a child, Joyce had a certain independence and precocity; there is a story of him at the age of four entertaining relatives who turned up unexpectedly, by playing the piano for them and singing.

John and May Joyce also visited their friends in Dublin, especially

The view of Bray Head and the Esplanade from Martello Terrace.

around Christmas and New Year, when they would go to dances and stay overnight at a hotel, just as Gabriel and Gretta Conroy do in 'The Dead'. In later life Stanislaus recounted how his mother would give the servants many anxious recommendations about their duties during her brief absence.

In their first year in Bray, John Joyce joined the Bray Boat Club, which was conveniently situated at the end of the Terrace at number 8. He resumed his interest in the manly sport of rowing, trained earnestly, and entered a regatta, rowing stroke in a four-man boat. In 1888 Bray Boat Club gave a public concert and the programme listed three members of the Joyce family; Mr J.S. Joyce, Mrs Joyce and Master James Joyce (then aged six).

May was kept busy in other ways too; between 4 July 1887 and 26 October 1891, she gave birth to four more children: George, Eileen, Mary and Eva. There were now eight children in the Joyce household.

Other relations stayed at Martello Terrace and came to be regarded as part of the family. These included John Joyce's maternal uncle from

Cork, William O'Connell, a tall, white haired man. He remained with the family for six years and appears in *A Portrait of the Artist as a Young Man* as 'Uncle Charles'. Another long-term guest was John Kelly, a colourful character from Tralee in County Kerry. He spent long sojourns with the family to recuperate from the effects of imprisonment from the part he played in the Land League agitation. He took a cold bath before attending mass each morning. He also helped May Joyce by doing the family shopping in Bray, accompanied by young Stanislaus. Like John Joyce, he was devoted to his country and to his chief, Charles Stewart Parnell, about whom they had endless discussions. John Kelly appears as Mr Casey in *A Portrait*.

It was a busy household. At any one time there could have been up to fifteen people staying in the house, which would have included the parents, eight children, William O'Connell, John Kelly, a nursemaid, a maid and another long-term guest, Mrs Conway.

Mrs Conway was an elderly relative of John Joyce. She was a clever, shrewd and bigoted woman who acted as governess to the children and in this capacity she started the education of Joyce. The children knew her as 'Dante', which is a child's pronunciation of 'Auntie'. Earlier she had been in a convent but left to get married when she inherited a large fortune. Two years later her husband went to South America, taking with him most of her money. Over the next few years, letters came from him less and less frequently until eventually they ceased altogether and he vanished leaving Mrs Conway a poor and embittered woman. This bitterness was shown in relation to Parnell when his liaison with Kitty O'Shea was revealed. Previously she had been an ardent follower of Parnell, the leader of the Irish Home Rule Party, going so far one evening as to hit a man with her umbrella because he took his hat off when the band on the esplanade played 'God Save the Queen'.

Dante sat, propped up by cushions to ease her ailing back, ('O, my back, my back, my bach! I'd want to go to Aches-les-Pains.' *Finnegans Wake*), wearing a heavy velvet skirt, jewelled slippers and a black lace

Charles Stewart Parnell.

cap. She was a well-read woman and taught Joyce reading, writing, arithmetic and geography, 'where the Mozambique Channel was and what was the longest river in America and what was the name of the highest mountain in the moon,' and she prepared him for his entrance to Clongowes Wood College, the principal Jesuit school in Ireland.

Joyce had a violent fear of thunderstorms, which remained with him all through his life. It was thought that Dante was responsible for this through the religious terror she instilled in him. She taught the children to cross themselves at every flash of lightning and repeat, 'Jesus of Nazareth, King of Jews, from a sudden and unprovided death deliver us, O Lord.'

James Vance, father of Joyce's childhood friend, Eileen. The Vance's lived at 4 Martello Terrace.

The waterfall in Powerscourt demesne, Enniskerry, a favourite picnic spot of the Joyce family.

Life in Bray was busy for the children. During the summer there were picnics at the waterfall in Powerscourt demesne in nearby Enniskerry, and at Christmas Dante brought the children to Dublin to see the crib at Inchicore, with its wax figures, later referred to in *Ulysses*.

Mr James Vance, a chemist, lived in number 4 Martello Terrace (not in number 7 as stated in *A Portrait*). He was of Huguenot origin, and, like John Joyce, came from Cork. Similar to John Joyce, he started his career as a medical student but gave up medicine and qualified as a pharmacist. He and John Joyce became friends and used to go fishing together. When Joyce was bitten by an excitable terrier on the esplanade, which resulted in his life long fear of dogs, it was Mr Vance who dressed his wounds. With his former medical training, allied to his pharmaceutical knowledge, he had the reputation of being, 'as good as any doctor'. Mr Vance had married sixteen-year-old Eleanor Atkinson when he was aged forty-five. They had three daughters, Eileen, Norah and Violet. He is remembered in *A Portrait* under his correct name, as is his daughter Eileen, who was only four months older than Joyce. Her oval face was framed by long red hair, which she wore in plaits. They both attended the same kindergarten, Miss Raynor's, in Seapoint Road, which is close to Martello Terrace. In an interview given by Eileen Vance (Mrs Harris) in 1953, she recalled her life in Bray. She said she knew nothing of Joyce's writings, until 1935 when she read *A Portrait of the Artist as a Young Man* and found that she was mentioned in it. She wrote to Joyce through his publishers, but he did not reply. She seemed rather incredulous when told that Joyce, whom she always called Jimmie, had exercised a very great influence on contemporary literature and that there was a constant and growing interest in his life and work.

As in *A Portrait*, both families were reasonably well-off. Martello Terrace was a fashionable neighbourhood then; she remembered nearby spacious terraces, with women playing tennis on the lawns and two or three servants in their homes. The two families were very close, especially the fathers and the children: 'We ran in and out of each other's homes all the time.' Her father and Joyce's father were both great singers, and they sang and drank together a great deal. They used to 'raise the roof' singing Irish 'Come-all-ye' songs. They especially liked songs in which Mr Vance (bass) and Mr Joyce (tenor) could contrast and blend their voices, as in 'The moon has raised her lamp above', and 'A soldier and a sailor'.

She did not realize as a small child how heavily Mr Joyce drank; not until she heard it from her father and aged sixteen or seventeen, when she visited the Joyce home in central Dublin and saw the miserable conditions in which they were living at 29 Windsor Terrace. She saw 'the bare boards and scrubbed planks' and to her it was a 'horrible place.' It was then that she realized that Mr Joyce had lost his job as a result of excessive drinking; 'he drank the whole family into destitution.' That year, Poppie was invited to come out to Bray for her summer holidays. She accepted the invitation and spent some time with Eileen.

She remembered Joyce's mother as a very beautiful woman, who had corn-coloured hair. She welcomed the little girl into her home and always had a kiss for her. The Joyce uncle was, 'a very pompous old gent.' He always wore a tall, silk hat and a cutaway coat. All she remembered of Aunt Dante was that Jimmie told her one day that his aunt had said if he did not give up playing with Eileen he would go to hell. This stuck in her mind, but apparently the threat did not frighten Jimmie because he continued to play with her.

She could recall no mention of the religious differences between the families. She spoke of family 'concerts' in the second-floor drawing-room of the Joyce home. The parents of the two families would assemble and watch the children 'dress up', play-act', sing, do games and skits. Jimmie organized the children for these affairs; he ruled the roost, he was leader in their play. Jimmie was as polite and well-behaved *vis-a-vis* her parents as she believed he was with his own parents.

She remembered a kindergarten school, Miss Raynor's in Bray, which Eileen, Norah, Jimmie and Poppie attended. She and Jimmie were always paired off together. It was taken for granted they would marry when they grew up. She believed that their fathers, in their good fellowship, must have started the idea of marrying their first born; at

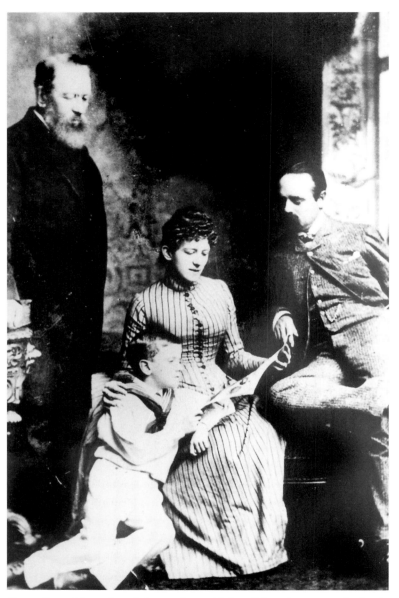

James Joyce, his mother, father and grandfather, John Murray, on the day he entered Clongowes Wood College, September 1888.

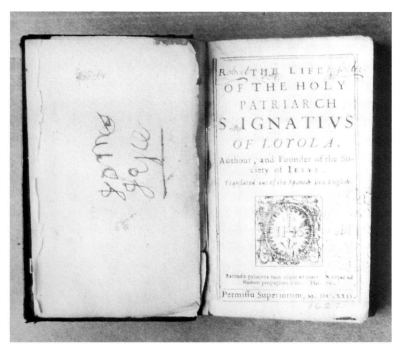

James Joyce's autograph, penned when he was aged six, on the flyleaf of the Life of St Ignatius Loyola, *printed in 1622.*

any rate, it was an understood thing among adults and children. Eileen carried the idea for years. She recalled that once in her early teens when she expressed admiration for some lad, Norah, her sister, exclaimed, 'But you can't look at him; you're going to marry Jimmie Joyce!'

Near St Valentine's Day of the first year Joyce was at Clongowes Wood, Eileen's father said to her, 'How about a Valentine for Jimmie?' He composed a verse for her and held her hand to help her to write:

> O Jimmie Joyce, you are my darling,
> You are my looking-glass from night till morning.
> I'd rather have you without a farthing
> Than Harry Newell and his ass and garden.

Harry Newell was a repulsive old cripple, who drove around Bray begging with a donkey and cart. He was the bugbear of the Vances, and perhaps the Joyce children too. When a child was naughty she was told, 'If you don't behave, I'll give you away to Harry Newell.' The Valentine was sent to Joyce at school.

As a child, Eileen believed that Jimmie was very clever and a little peculiar. He had a vivid imagination and would make up the most fantastic tales and tell them to her in deadly seriousness; for years she believed everything he told her. She recalled one example because it had scared her: when the children were naughty, Jimmie said that his mother would hold them head downwards in the toilet bowl and pull the chain! After that, although she liked Mrs Joyce, she was always careful to be good in her neighbourhood. Jimmie also had his own way of punishing his younger brothers and sisters when they displeased him. He had a red stocking cap, which he put on, and the offending child was made to lie on the ground with a little red wheelbarrow put over him. Jimmie was now the Devil and made sounds to indicate that the offender under the wheelbarrow was being burned in hell.

It was during Poppie's summer holiday in Bray that Eileen saw Jimmie for the last time. She was then about sixteen or seventeen. Jimmie and his father came out to Bray one afternoon, but he and Eileen had no serious talk. Jimmie, tall and slight, just sat and stared at her, as if appraising the girl she had become.

The Vances moved from Martello Terrace to live over their chemist shop at 92 Main Street, Bray. The shop, now owned by Michael Kennedy, still trades under the name Vance & Wilson.

Martello Terrace is important in the Joycean canon because it was here that Joyce spent his early formative years; years in which he developed an acute facility for observation, for remembering conversations and events, which occurred around him. His early impressions were vivid and lasting.

II
Schooldays:
Clongowes Wood
to Belvedere College,
1888–98

JOHN JOYCE wanted the very best available education for his eldest son and that is why he chose Clongowes Wood College in Sallins, County Kildare. The name Clongowes Wood is first mentioned in 1417, in a Close Roll of King Henry IV. In 1450 an Anglo-Norman family named Eustace built the castle at Clongowes Wood and remained there until the rebellion of 1641, when their castle was destroyed by General Monck. After the Restoration the Eustace family did not regain their estates; in 1667 Charles II granted Clongowes, situated on a thousand acres, to Sir Richard Reynell. He in turn sold it to a Dublin barrister named Thomas Browne and the name was changed to Castle Browne. On his death, his brother, Michael Wogan Browne, inherited the property. In March 1814 it was purchased by Father Peter Kenney, SJ, who had to get around the anti-Catholic penal laws by buying it in his own name rather than on behalf of the Jesuit Order. That same year it opened as a school.

Every castle has its story, and Clongowes Wood is no exception. Joyce incorporates in his works a couple of the historic events which took place at Clongowes Wood. A member of the Browne family, who was a marshal in the Austrian army, took part in the Battle of Prague,

1757, where he was killed. It is said that at the precise moment of his death he was seen by his servants in the castle as he walked up the stairs, clad in his blood-stained white uniform. In *A Portrait*, Stephen Dedalus finds it cold and strange to think that 'There were pale strange faces there, great eyes like carriage lamps… They were the ghosts of murderers, the figures of marshals who had received their death-wound on battlefields far away over the sea.'

Another event took place in 1794 when Hamilton Rowan, a patriot and friend of Wolfe Tone, fled to the castle after he was accused of rebellion. He entered the castle as the soldiers were firing, so that their bullets hit the door. There he threw his hat on the ha-ha as a decoy to fool his pursuers. They thought he had left and he later made good his escape to France. Joyce was so intrigued and impressed by Rowan's method of evading his pursuers that he named the protagonist in his play, *Exiles*, Richard Rowan.

August 1888 was a momentous month for Joyce. He was the centre of attention in the Joyce household as preparations were underway to

The main entrance of Clongowes Wood College.

get him organized for school. His parents took him to town to get him all the items he needed for his first trunk, which was initialled J.A.J. He required three suits of clothes, a flannel cricket shirt, six shirts, eight pairs of stockings, four pillow cases, boots and house shoes.

According to his brother Stanislaus, Joyce enjoyed being the centre of such preparations He always liked new adventure, new scenes, and the illusion of stability never seduced him, as was evident throughout his life.

Joyce's fourteen years' education with the Jesuits was about to begin. It would include Clongowes Wood, in County Kildare, and Belvedere College and University College in Dublin. On 1 September 1888 Joyce travelled with his parents on the forty-mile journey from Bray to Clongowes Wood, situated in a beautiful woodland setting, two miles north-east of the Liffey-side village of Clane. They took the train from Bray to Dublin, and then continued by train from Kingsbridge to Sallins, a journey that took less than an hour. Travelling the last three and a half miles by horse drawn car to the college, they entered the main gateway and drove up the formidable, tree-lined drive to the school: 'A long shiver of fear flowed over his body. He saw the dark entrance hall of the castle.'

The fee was forty guineas a year, payable half-yearly on 1 September and 1 February with an added five pounds for miscellaneous items such as washing and the repair of clothing. However, for the first two years of his son's attendance at Clongowes Wood, John Joyce was charged only twenty-two pounds per annum, which included everything. This was probably because Joyce was only six-and-a-half years old and was by far the youngest and smallest boy in the school. Nevertheless, it was quite an amount in those days to invest in the education of a small boy.

On arrival at the college, Mr and Mrs Joyce and their son were welcomed by the courteous and kindly Father Conmee, SJ, described in *A Portrait* as 'the decentest rector that was ever in Clongowes Wood'.

Father Conmee came to Clongowes as prefect of studies, and in 1885, at the age of thirty-eight, was appointed rector. Stephen's red-eyed mother tells him not to speak with the rough boys at the college and his father advises him not to inform on another boy and gives him two five-shilling pieces for his pocket money, before the rector shakes hands with them at the castle door.

Similarities exist between what actually happened to Joyce at Clongowes Wood and what is recounted by Stephen Dedalus in *A Portrait*. Stephen goes to the rector's office to complain about being unjustly treated when he is pandied by Father Dolan for breaking his glasses on the cinder-path. Stephen refers to the 'rector's kind-looking face'; Father Conmee had listened sympathetically to him. Father Conmee appears in *Ulysses* when an account is given of his journey from his presbytery in Dublin to the suburb of Artane. He became the Superior of the Jesuit residence in Upper Gardiner Street on 24 October 1898, and coincidentally, his term there finished on 16 June 1904, the day on which *Ulysses* is set.

Being so young, Joyce did not sleep in the dormitory with the other boys, but had a room in the infirmary, where he was cared for by Nanny Galvin. He was also under the supervision of Brother Hanly for his first two years at Clongowes Wood.

A few months after he entered the school, the Minister and Prefect of Health, Father Thomas Brown, wrote to Mrs Joyce to say that James had written her a letter, but had not given the letter to be posted. He added that Joyce was well and that he had been taking his cod-liver oil regularly.

The small, thin boy with the light-blue eyes remembered the tide washing against the sea-wall at his home in Bray as he knelt in the college chapel. 'It was cold and dark under the sea-wall beside his father's house, but the kettle would be on the hob to make punch.'

The square ditch may still be seen at Clongowes Wood. It was into this that Wells shoved Stephen because he would not swop his little snuff box for Wells' hacking chestnut.

It is interesting to note that some of the students at school with Stephen in *A Portrait* share the names of the boys who were contemporaries or classmates of Joyce. Out of the twenty-two names listed in the first chapter, fifteen can be traced. The eight boys from Dublin are: Rudolph Kickham, John Cantwell, Cecil Thunder, Charles Wells, James Magee, Stanislaus Little, Alexander Kickham and Thomas Furlong. Other contemporaries were John Lawton, from Midleton (appears as Jack Lawton); Michael Saurin, from Youghal (appears as Fleming); Patrick Rath, from Enniscorthy and Argentina; Jose Arana y Lupardo, from Bilbao, Spain (appears as the Spaniard) and Dominick Kelly, from Waterford.

One of the pupils of Clongowes, Stanislaus Little, died on 10 December 1890, and his grave is to the left of the gate inside the Jesuit cemetery. It is marked by a white cross which bears the inscription, 'Sacred to the memory of Peter Stanislaus Little who died 10 December 1890 aged sixteen years.' In *A Portrait*, as Stephen lies ill in the infirmary, he thinks he may die before his mother comes, and he ponders on the death and funeral of Stanislaus Little; and wonders if he would be buried like Little, in the small cemetery off the main avenue of limes.

The Jesuits who appear in *A Portrait* have their real-life counterparts; Brother Hanly appears as Brother Michael; Father William Power appears as Father Arnall; Father James Daly appears as Father Dolan and Father Conmee appears under his own name as does Mr William Gleeson, a member of the Jesuit community, who was studying for his matriculation examination for the Royal University.

At Clongowes Wood, there were two vacations in the year, eight weeks in the summer and three weeks at Christmas. In 1891, when Joyce was home for Christmas holidays, the events which are recounted so vividly in *A Portrait*, concerning the Christmas dinner, took place. This illustrates the influence his early years had on his works. Guests at the dinner table included John Kelly (Mr Casey); Mrs Conway (Mrs Riordan/Dante) and William O'Connell (Uncle Charles). A heated discussion, which became rancorous, arose during the meal, concerning Parnell who had died shortly before on 6 October. Dante had been accurate when she had said, 'Oh, he'll remember all this when he grows up…the language he heard against God and religion and priests in his own home.'

Around this time, John Joyce lost his job in the Office of the Collector of Rates and the salary of five hundred pounds per annum. He was forty-two years of age and would have had no pension if his wife had not intervened with the authorities, who finally agreed to pay him a pension of £132. 2s. 4d. a year. He never held another position and his financial state fell rapidly into decline. The rents he made on his Cork properties were taken up by the interest on the mortgages.

At the start of Joyce's third and last year at Clongowes Wood, the fee went up and John Joyce was required to pay the full amount, which totalled £23. 17s. in October 1890, and £25. 17s. 9d. in February 1891. These were the last bills John Joyce was to pay for his son's education. Joyce was withdrawn from the school in December 1892, although it was strongly recommended in the school prospectus that, as far as possible, boys should be moved only at the summer vacation.

Early in 1892 the family, accompanied by Mrs Conway and William O'Connell, moved again to a large house called Leoville, at 23 Carysfort Avenue, in Blackrock. Like Bray, Blackrock is a maritime town. Situated five miles from the city centre, it had a good transport system with tramcars arriving from and starting for Dublin every fifteen minutes. There was also a train every half an hour. The population was about nine thousand and there were a lot of summer visitors who came to swim at the Blackrock Baths, which are no longer in use. These were situated beside the station. The Joyces had as neighbours a doctor, a grocer, a spirit merchant, a newsagent, a fishmonger and a greengrocer. The house is situated on a corner at the junction of Carysfort Avenue and Frescati Road. This road formerly linked Rock Hill and Carysfort Avenue ending in a T-junction, but it now extends and forms a new

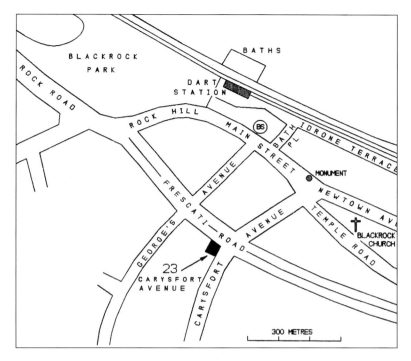

highway, by-passing the village of Blackrock (see map). This alters the area completely, with traffic passing alongside the house. It is not the peaceful suburban road it was when the Joyces lived there. Built in the 1840s, the semi-detached house is a spacious end-of-terrace residence with an impressive original façade; but it has been altered considerably at the rear, with extensions added at different periods. It is two-storey on the front and three-storey at the back, with a fine view of Howth Head and Dublin Bay from an east-facing upstairs window. There is a slated granite entrance porch with Georgian pillars and canopy that forms a portico. A stone lion crouched on top of this portico, from which the house derived its name, Leoville.

The beautiful stained-glass panels of Dante and Beatrice, which were in the hall door were removed by a later owner. Inside, there is an unusually large entrance hall which has a fireplace. There are two large

Carysfort Avenue, Blackrock.

'Leoville', 23 Carysfort Avenue.

reception rooms at ground-floor level, one incorporating a stained-glass fanlight. On the first floor, a large drawing-room spans the front of the house, incorporating the three large windows. It measures thirty feet by ten feet, six inches. There are two bedrooms at this level and two on the third storey. The back garden has been shortened considerably. A plaque on the wall commemorates Joyce's years here. In 'A Painful Case', Mrs Emily Sinico lives in Leoville, Sydney Parade Avenue, Ballsbridge.

Two more daughters were born at this address; Florence, in 1892, and Mabel, in 1893, bringing the number of children to ten. It was probably here that Joyce wrote his poem titled 'Et Tu Healy!' which his father had printed as a broadside by the firm of Alleyn and O'Reilly. No copies are known to have survived. It concerns Timothy Healy, later to become the first Governor-General of the Irish Free State, who turned against Parnell at the time of his downfall. In *A Portrait*, the day after the discussion on Parnell at the Christmas dinner table, Stephen sees himself trying to compose a poem about Parnell. Stanislaus said that Joyce wrote it when he was aged between nine and ten years old, and he was positive that the broadside was printed when they were living in Blackrock. He remembered his father bringing home a roll of thirty or forty of them and giving them to his friends.

It was at this time that Joyce's ambition to be a writer bore its first blossom. He wrote poetry and essays, and with his next door neighbour, a Protestant boy named Raynod, who was a year or so older than himself, he started to write a novel. The pair used to discuss it, then Joyce would retreat and spend the afternoon writing at the big leather-covered desk in the corner of the dining-room. None of these manuscripts survived.

Uncle William used to read fairy-tales from Grimm and Andersen to the children, but Joyce read on his own. All the children of school-going age, with the exception of James, attended Sion Hill, the local convent school on Mount Merrion Avenue. Joyce stayed at home studying and his mother heard his lessons. Every evening, in the conservatory at the back of the house, Dante used to preside at the Rosary and the Litany of the Blessed Virgin.

In *A Portrait*, Uncle Charles and Stephen were constant companions during the summer months in Blackrock. Uncle Charles smoked a strong-smelling tobacco and repaired to the shed at the end of the garden, which he shared with the cat and the garden tools, to have his few puffs. He would then go with Stephen to do the shopping in the main street of the town. Uncle Charles was good to Stephen, giving him helpings of items, which were in open boxes outside the counter, while the shopkeeper smiled uneasily in the background. They would then repair to Blackrock Park where Mike Flynn, a friend of Stephen's father, would be waiting for them seated on a bench; the child would practise long-distance running under his professional eye. He had heard his father say that 'Mike Flynn had put some of the best runners of modern times through his hands'.

Blackrock Park is much the same as when Joyce used it as a child. With the construction of the first railway in 1834, which ran from Dublin to Kingstown (now Dun Laoghaire), the area between the track and Rock Road became a marsh. With the application of the Towns Improvement Act to the locality, the swamp was transformed into a formal Victorian Park, which was ready for public use in 1883. Built on an incline, it is nicely landscaped with rockeries, flowering trees and shrubs and contains two small lakes. Since 1930 it has been under the care of the Corporation of Dun Laoghaire, now Dun Laoghaire Rathdown County Council.

After their visit to the park, Uncle Charles and Stephen would pay a visit to the church in Blackrock where Uncle Charles would pray… Stephen often wondered, was he praying that God might send him back part of his squandered Cork fortune? At weekends, Stephen would accompany his father, Simon Dedalus, and Uncle Charles on interesting long walks through the green lanes of Stillorgan and the Goatstown Road, then on to Dundrum and back through Sandyford.

Blackrock Park.

These were long walks for a child but perhaps a pony and trap could have conveyed them part of the journey. For some time the boy had sensed slight changes in the house. He felt his father was in trouble... whispers here and there... he was not to return to Clongowes Wood. All of these incidences were taken from Joyce's own experiences.

In *My Brother's Keeper*, Stanislaus recounted that he had a few scattered but significant memories of that brief interlude between relative prosperity and real poverty. He recalled returning from the shoreline in Blackrock, where he had been playing with his friends, and seeing his father, quite drunk but still elegant, playing a piano-organ in the main street of the town and crooning 'The Boys of Wexford', while the organ-grinder looked on in amazement.

Dante left the family and went to live with various friends, never staying too long with any one of them as she could never again find a family who would put up with her dictatorial manner as the Joyce family had done. She had taken Poppie, the eldest daughter at almost nine years, with her and succeeded in making the child's life a 'careless round of tedious duties'. A few years later, Dante, who had so much influence on the young Joyce, died of fatty degeneration of the heart. William O'Connell, who had been a friend to the Joyce family and especially the children, left and returned to Cork.

In the first draft of *A Portrait*, entitled *Stephen Hero*, the poem 'Et Tu Healy' was ascribed to this period. Joyce refers to the remaining broadsides, of which young Stephen had been so proud, lying torn on the floor and muddied by the boots of the removal men, who had hustled the furniture out through the front garden 'which was strewn with wisps of straw and rope ends and into the huge vans at the gate.' Disintegration had set in abruptly. John Joyce, accompanied by his wife and ten children, left Blackrock at the end of 1892 or early 1893, amid the clamour of a threatening landlord and dunning creditors. The reason for the move was John Joyce's repugnance at paying rent. In *A Portrait*, it is related how Stephen and his mother could see from the window of their railway carriage, two great yellow caravans with their furniture lumbering heavily along the Merrion Road.

The vans deposited their loads at their new lodgings at 29 Hardwicke Street, where they remained for some months. This street, which was laid out about 1805–07, was named after the third Earl, who was Lord Lieutenant of Ireland. Most of it was demolished by the Corporation in 1954 for new blocks of flats. Maurice Craig, in his book *Dublin 1660–1860*, gives two descriptions of this area; in 1820 Thomas Cromwell wrote: 'the streets in the vicinity are all built on a regular plan: the houses are lofty and elegant; and neither hotels, shops, nor warehouses, obtruding upon the scene, the whole possesses an air of dignified retirement – the tranquillity of ease, affluence and leisure. The inhabitants of this parish are indeed almost exclusively of the upper ranks…'

In 1894, when the Joyces lived there, Somerville and Ross in *The Real Charlotte*, gave this description of an August Sunday afternoon:

Tall brick houses, browbeating each other in gloomy respectability across the white streets; broad pavements, promenaded mainly by the nomadic cat; stifling squares, where the in-fant of unfashionable parentage is taken for the daily baking that is substitute for the breezes and the press of perambulators on the Bray Esplanade or the Kingstown pier. Few towns are duller out of the season than Dublin, but the dullness of its north side neither waxes nor wanes... So at least it appears to the observer whose impressions are only eye-deep, and are derived from the emptiness of the streets, the unvarying dirt of the window panes, and the almost forgotten type of ugliness of the window curtains.

Joyce's story 'The Boarding House' is set in Waverley House, 4 Hardwicke Street, at the intersection of Frederick Court. This was the only boarding house listed in the street consisting of forty-eight houses and it is still in existence.

The next move was to a large house, possibly the largest that the family inhabited. It was 14 Fitzgibbon Street, named for John Fitzgibbon, Earl of Clare. Fitzgibbon Street slopes east from Mountjoy Square, towards the North Circular Road. This sombre, grey, eighteenth-century house was four-storeys over a basement with stone steps leading up to a front door, which had a fanlight and attendant pillars. It comprised two rooms in the basement, sub-divided into a kitchen, wine-cellar and butler's pantry. The ground floor consisted of an entrance hall, stairway, morning room and sitting-room. On the first floor was an elaborately decorated drawing-room, spanning the width of the house, and two back rooms. The second floor had three bedrooms, two at the front and one at the back, and the top floor had four, which would have originally been the servants quarters. A number of the houses along the street had ironwork balconies outside their first floor, street-facing drawing-rooms. In *Ulysses* Stephen refers to his father Simon Dedalus kindling a fire in an unfurnished room in the house.

14 Fitzgibbon Street (renumbered as 34), probably the largest house the Joyce family inhabited and their last 'good' address.

The family remained in Fitzgibbon Street for over a year. At the time it was a residential area for well-off families, and it was the last of the Joyces' good addresses. The neighbours consisted of a law agent, contractor, composer and professor of music. As in *A Portrait*, Joyce, was becoming slowly aware that his father had enemies and that some fight was about to take place, in which he would be enlisted. He began to understand why the servants were whispering in the hallway:

> Dublin was a new and complex sensation...the sudden flight from the comfort and revery of Blackrock, the passage through the gloomy foggy city, the thought of the bare cheerless house in which they were now to live made his heart heavy. He timidly explored the neighbourhood and passed unchallenged along the docks and quays. The vastness and strangeness of this new bustling life amazed him... he was embittered and angry with himself for being young and the prey of restless foolish impulses, angry also with the change of fortune which was reshaping the world about him into a vision of squalor and insincerity.

Mr Dedalus assures Stephen, 'We're not dead yet, sonny. No, by the Lord Jesus (God forgive me), not half dead.'

This move from airy Blackrock to the city centre was a turning-point. In the *Partisan Review*, Stanislaus wrote, 'The rapid down-hill slide to almost abject poverty began when we left Blackrock for Dublin.'

From Fitzgibbon Street, Joyce would visit his favourite relative, his aunt Josephine Murray, who lived in Drumcondra just over a mile away. She was the wife of William Murray, a brother of Joyce's mother, and she always lent a sympathetic ear to Joyce. He corresponded with her throughout her life. From Fitzgibbon Street Stephen, in *A Portrait*, also went with his mother to visit relatives. Passing shops festive for Christmas, 'The causes of his embitterment were many, remote and near.' At a party in Harold's Cross Stephen felt himself gloomy among the other guests. The next day he sat in the bare room of the house in front of his desk, with green exercise book and ink-bottle, daydreaming about Bray and the time he tried to write a poem about Parnell.

The children did not attend school for some months and Joyce spent much of this time, often whole days, wandering around and exploring the city, sometimes with Stanislaus at his heels. He chronicled in his subconscious the places which he encountered during these peregrinations and became familiar with the topography of the Dublin streets. Like Stephen, 'He had his ears and eyes ever prompt to receive impressions. It was not only in Skeat that he found words for his treasure house, he found them at hazard in the shops, in advertisements, in the mouths of the plodding public. He kept repeating them to himself until they lost all instantaneous meaning for him and became wonderful vocables.' John Joyce said of his son, 'If that fellow was dropped on the middle of the Sahara, he'd sit, be God, and make a map of it.'

From Fitzgibbon Street, Joyce and Stanislaus attended the O'Connell Christian Brothers school in North Richmond Street for a few months. Stephen in *A Portrait* does not; John Joyce, like Mr Dedalus, never liked the idea of sending Stephen to the school, saying that if he started with the Jesuits, he could stick with them:

> —I never liked the idea of sending him to the christian brothers myself, said Mrs Dedalus.
> —Christian brothers bedamned! said Mr Dedalus. Is it with Paddy Stink and Micky Mud? No, let him stick to the jesuits in God's name since he began with them.

A fortuitous meeting between John Joyce and the influential Father Conmee at the corner of Mountjoy Square led in Joyce continuing with the Jesuits after a break of fifteen months. Conmee had left his position as rector of Clongowes Wood to become Prefect of Studies at Belvedere College. Hearing Joyce was obliged to attend the Christian Brothers due to his father's declining fortunes, and remembering his former pupil's diligence and ability, he kindly agreed to accept both Joyce and his brother Stanislaus into Belvedere without payment of fees.

—I walked bang into him, said Mr Dedalus for the fourth time, just at the corner of the square.

—Then I suppose, said Mrs Dedalus, he will be able to arrange it. I mean about Belvedere.

Father John S. Conmee, SJ.

Belvedere House in Great Denmark Street, which faces down the hill of North Great George's Street, is one of the finest eighteenth-century houses in Dublin. It was built by Michael Stapleton in 1786, for George Rochfort, the second Earl of Belvedere, and purchased, for the Jesuits in 1841. Three years later the Jesuits purchased, for expansion purposes, the adjoining house, which had been the town house of Lord Fingall. A hall, which served both for a gymnasium and a theatre, was built in the garden of the house. Belvedere House contains a remarkable variety of decorative plasterwork, executed by Stapleton, which includes stylised birds in the Venus room and antlered stags in lunettes in the Diana room. An unusual feature is the double frieze on the staircase and the decorated plasterwork underneath it. As he did with Clongowes Wood, Joyce researched the history of the Belvedere family, and refers briefly to it in *Ulysses*.

Belvedere College was only a five-minute walk from the Joyce home in Fitzgibbon Street. It has changed little since the serious and rather observant boy, then aged eleven, entered the College in III Grammar with his brother Stanislaus entering Elements, on 6 April 1893. In September of the same year Joyce entered the Preparatory Grade and his education started in earnest. During his five years at Belvedere and with the increasing household turmoil, he took learning in his stride.

He was a brilliant student, mastering Italian, French and Latin and excelling in English composition. His English teacher, George Dempsey, who appears as Mr Tate in *A Portrait*, noticed his extraordinary talent and pointed him out to the Prefect of Studies as a boy with 'a plethora of ideas in his head'. When Joyce went into higher classes, Dempsey would read out his compositions to serve as examples to the rest of the class. Poverty was grinding the family, and John Joyce was becoming more desperate in regard to financial matters. This led to a trip to Cork in February 1894, when Joyce and his father went to sell the remainder of the mortgaged properties. Like Stephen and Mr Dedalus in *A Portrait*,

Belvedere College which Joyce attended for five years.

they took the night-mail train from Kingsbridge Station (now Heuston): 'he saw the darkening lands slipping away past him, the silent telegraph-poles passing his window swiftly every four seconds...'

They stayed in the Imperial Hotel and visited places of John Joyce's bygone youth, where Joyce was assured that his father was 'the handsomest man in Cork at that time, by God he was! The women used to stand to look after him in the street' and 'the boldest flirt in the City of Cork in his day.' They visited the Mardyke, which was once a fine promenade, and Queen's College, now University College Cork, where Joyce inspected the desk where his father had carved his initials some thirty years previously and where he had made an abortive attempt to become a doctor, having entered in 1867 and passed his first-year examination in medicine. He had devoted his time not to study, but to college theatricals and sport. Joyce and his father visited the pretty seaside town of Crosshaven, where John Joyce called on the nuns in the Presentation Convent in the hope of gaining admittance for his daughters as free boarders to the school.

A substantial sum was made from the sale of the Cork properties which included buildings at 7 and 8 Angelsea Street, as well as premises in White Street. Two months previously, fourteen-hundred pounds had been raised by an auction of property and ground at the rear of South Terrace, and by an auction of property and coach-house in Stable Lane. In *A Portrait*, it states: 'On the evening of the day on which the property was sold Stephen followed his father meekly about the city from bar to bar.' The Cork journey proved of no financial gain whatsoever to John Joyce, but only to his creditor, the Dublin solicitor and money-lender, Reuben J. Dodd, who appears briefly in *Ulysses*. The denuding of his father's pockets to pay back heavy debts to Dodd rankled deeply with Joyce, particularly since Dodd's son was his contemporary at Belvedere College.

The Joyce family now had a pension of eleven pounds per month to survive on, together with what John Joyce could earn from odd jobs such as canvassing advertisements for the *Freeman's Journal*, as Leopold Bloom does in *Ulysses*, or working as a scrivener for a solicitor on the quays. At election time, he was employed in different capacities, such as revising voting lists or acting as presiding officer at municipal elections. But whatever money he did make was not usually spent on his family.

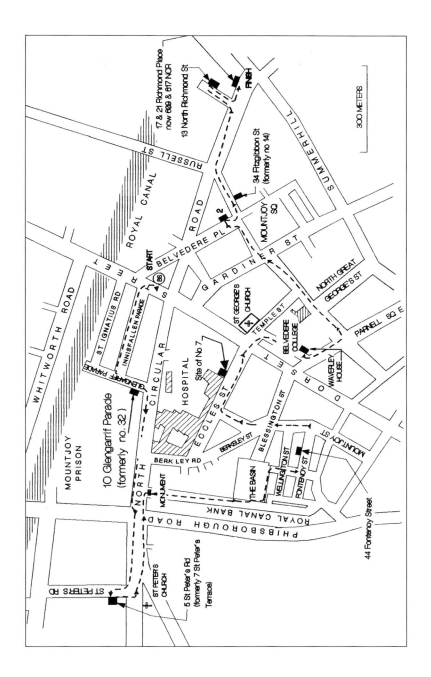

The map contains the following labels:

WHITWORTH ROAD

MOUNTJOY PRISON

10 Glengarrif Parade (formerly no. 32)

ST IGNATIUS RD

INNISFALLEN PARADE

GLENGARRIF PARADE

NORTH CIRCULAR ROAD

ROYAL CANAL

RUSSELL ST

START

86

BELVEDERE PL

17 & 21 Richmond Place now 609 & 617 NCR

13 North Richmond St

FINISH

34 Fitzgibbon St (formerly no 14)

2

GARDINER ST

MOUNTJOY SQ

SUMMERHILL

ROAD

ST GEORGE'S CHURCH

TEMPLE ST

NORTH GREAT GEORGE'S ST

PARNELL SQ E

BELVEDERE COLLEGE

WAVERLEY HOUSE

DORSET ST

HOSPITAL

Site of No 7

ECCLES ST

BERKELEY ST

BLESSINGTON ST

MOUNTJOY ST

BERKELEY RD

MONUMENT

THE BASIN

WELLINGTON ST

PORTBHOY ST

ROYAL CANAL BANK

PHIBSBOROUGH ROAD

44 Fontenoy Street

ST PETER'S RD

ST PETER'S CHURCH

ST PETER'S Rd

5 St Peter's Rd (formerly 7 St Peter's Terrace)

300 METERS

2 Millbourne Avenue, Drumcondra, the Joyces' seventh home, demolished in 1998.

He was quite unburdened by any sense of responsibility towards them.

At the beginning of March 1894 John Joyce was forced to move with his wife and ten children to their seventh home, 2 Millbourne Avenue, Drumcondra, which was not far from where they were already living. It is situated two miles north of the city centre, up the wide and spacious Dorset Street and Drumcondra Road, which were originally on the route of one of the four great roads of ancient Ireland, the Slighe Mhidhluachra, that entered the city from the north.

In 1894 the Drumcondra area had a population of eight thousand. The Roman Catholic Missionary College of All-Hallows, which educated clergy for foreign missions, was close by. Having crossed Drumcondra Bridge, which spans the River Tolka, Millbourne Avenue is the second turn to the left and is sandwiched between Millmount Avenue and the high walls which border the grounds of St Patrick's Teacher Training College. When the Joyces lived here, there was only Millbourne Avenue and it was the first turn to the left after the bridge. In *A Portrait*, Stephen crosses the bridge and looks towards the statue of the Blessed Virgin, which stood fowl-wise on a pole in the middle of a ham-shaped encampment of poor cottages. He bends to the left, following the lane that led up to his house. On his way he passes two dairies and a gardener's cottage and smells the rotted cabbages from the kitchen gardens on the rising ground above the river. He thinks of the garden behind his own house and the solitary farm-hand whom the children referred to as 'the man with the hat'. It was a semi-rural area, with many of the neighbours making a living from small dairies and also working as cattle-dealers, farm-hands, and gardeners. Some navvies lived in a row of run-down cottages. The Joyce house, which was semi-detached, was formerly known as Holywell Villas, so called after the nearby St Catherine's Well. It was situated at the top right-hand side of Millbourne Avenue. It contained two reception rooms, a kitchen and three bedrooms, and was built for letting in the late 1880s by a Mr Butterly. It was described by Stanislaus as 'a small semi-detached villa, almost in the country, at the foot of a low hill'. The low hill has since been built upon with a corporation housing estate and the incline referred to is now Ferguson Road. Nearby there were fields and woods and a weir into the River Tolka, where Joyce used to trespass with his school friends. This area is now incorporated into Griffith Park. 2 Millbourne Avenue was demolished in November 1998.

The Joyce family, who had obviously known better times, were not welcomed by their neighbours, especially the children, who tended to pick fights with them. This usually happened when the young Joyces were on their way home from school; they had to pass by the cottages, and then the catcalling and stone-throwing from the opposition would commence. Stanislaus was the first to be accosted when he fought with a red-headed rough-neck, with the evocative name of Pisser Duffy. In the story, 'A Painful Case', Stanislaus served as the model for the hero whom Joyce gave the name Duffy. Stanislaus was unfortunate enough

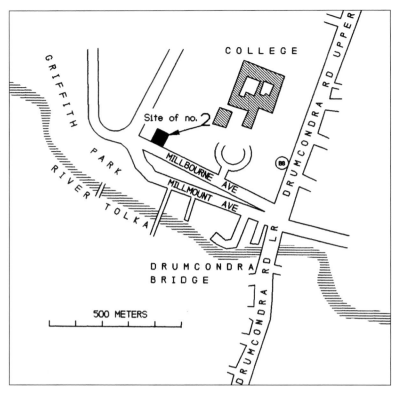

to be spotted with a group of his schoolmates on the bank of the Royal Canal by Father Henry, the rector of Belvedere, when he was about to engage in a fight with the enemy group. The following day he was reprimanded by him in Latin class and, when asked what he had been doing the previous day on the canal bank, he replied 'Nothing, sir.' Father Henry retorted 'Do you call it nothing to go fighting ragamuffins on the canal bank?'

Griffith Park, directly opposite 2 Millbourne Avenue, is where Joyce was beaten up by three of his schoolmates, who were envious of his achievements with his school themes. This incident is recounted in *A Portrait* when Stephen is beaten by Heron, Nash and Nolan because he would not agree with them that Tennyson was a better poet than the immoral and heretical Byron. Joyce was flung against a barbedwire fence and his already shabby clothes were ripped. According to Stanislaus, the discussion about Byron and heresy and the tussle with three of his classmates in *A Portrait* is neither invented nor exaggerated. This was one of the unpleasant memories of their Drumcondra address.

Stanislaus described Millbourne Avenue as 'Bleak House' and in *A Portrait*, Stephen Dedalus describes a scene that illustrates their steady decline in living standards from the halcyon days in Bray, when he wore his Eton jacket and the servants placed the dishes on the table before him:

> He pushed open the latchless door of the porch and passed through the naked hallway into the kitchen. A group of his brothers and sisters was sitting around the table. Tea was nearly over and only the last of the second watered tea remained in the bottoms of the small glass jars and jampots which did service for teacups. Discarded crusts and lumps of sugared bread, turned brown by the tea which had been poured over them, lay scattered on the table. Little wells of tea lay here and there on the board, and a knife with a broken ivory handle was stuck through the pith of a ravaged turnover.

When he enquired where his father and mother were he was told, ' —Goneboro toboro lookboro atboro aboro houseboro.'

Despite the disordered household, Joyce did well at Belvedere College, winning one of the top prizes in the Intermediate Examination, which was held in the spring on 1894. All the schools in Ireland competed in the Preparatory Grade, and the prize was twenty pounds, which was paid by the government to John Joyce. Like Mr Dedalus in *A Portrait*, they had collected the money in the Bank of Ireland at Foster Place in October with a keen wind blowing around: 'Stephen looked at his thinly-clad mother and remembered that a few days before he had seen a mantle priced twenty guineas in the windows of Barnardo's.' Barnardo & Son, furriers, is still at 108 Grafton Street. His father gave the money over to Joyce to spend it as he liked. In doing so, he thought it would teach him the value of money. The twelve-year-old Joyce took his parents to expensive restaurants and to the theatre. He bought practical presents for his brothers and sisters; a pair of boots for one, a dress for another. When the money was spent, the household returned to its usual way of life.

After his summer examinations at Belvedere, which commenced on 12 June 1894, Joyce accompanied his father on a journey to Glasgow. The ship's captain, who was a friend of John Joyce, offered him a free trip. On the return journey a heated argument took place concerning Parnell: 'By God, man, if he had been drinking he would have thrown me overboard' John Joyce often related later.

In spite of the miasmic gloom of their life in Millbourne Avenue, Stanislaus described happy family picnics, and swimming at Howth and the Bull Wall, and of times when all the children sat around singing in the house:

> The voice of the younger brother from the farther side of the fireplace began to sing the air 'Oft in the Stilly Night.' One by one the others took up the air until a full choir of voices was singing. They would sing so for hours, melody after melody, glee after glee, till the last pale light died down on the horizon, till the first dark night clouds came forth and night fell.

May Joyce gave birth in the early autumn to her eleventh child, a son named Freddie, who sadly survived only a few weeks. John Joyce's short temper became shorter. He became violent and grabbed his wife catching her by the throat and roared, 'Now, by God, is the time to finish it.' The children screamed and tried to separate them. Finally Joyce jumped on his father's back and pulled them to the ground, thus enabling his mother to escape with her daughters to a neighbour's house. A few days later a policeman called to their home and had a long talk with Mr and Mrs Joyce. Mrs Joyce thought of getting a separation but received quite an unsympathetic ear from the parish priest.

In September 1894 Joyce started his second year and Junior Grade at Belvedere College. J.F. Byrne and Vincent Cosgrave, who appeared respectively as Cranly and Lynch in *A Portrait*, were in his class. In all, he named ten pupils from Belvedere in this book. Vincent Heron who was Stephen's rival is the most obvious and he was a merging of two brothers, Vincent and Albrecth Connolly.

At home, unpaid bills were accumulating at an alarming rate, the landlord was dunning for his rent, and in late 1894, or early 1895, the family was on the move again, back across the Tolka and Royal Canal to 13 North Richmond Street. Ironically, the last person to wish them godspeed was Pisser Duffy's father, who was brought in to the dismantled parlour, and over a bottle of stout expressed his regret for past misunderstandings and offered the good wishes of the cottagers.

North Richmond Street is much the same now as it was when the Joyces lived there, except the numbers one to three have been demolished and the O'Connell school, which Joyce and Stanislaus had once attended for a short spell, has been rebuilt and extended. The area was therefore familiar ground to both Joyce and Stanislaus. It is a cul-de-sac, and is thus described in 'Araby': 'An uninhabited house of two-storeys stood at the blind end, detached from its neighbours... the other houses of the street... gazed at one another with brown imperturbable faces.'

The three-storey house, which was located on the east side of the street, had high, cold, empty, gloomy rooms. The basement comprised a kitchen and pantry area. In *Ulysses* Stephen Dedalus recalls his mother lighting a fire in the kitchen in 1898 on the morning of the feast of St Francis Xavier. On the ground floor there was a hallway with two

13 North Richmond Street. This house and the surrounding area received a lot of attention in Joyce's work.

rooms off it. There were two rooms each on the second and third floors, with the bathroom on the second-floor return. There was a garden at the back, which had a central apple-tree and a few straggling bushes.

The family remained here for four years, their longest period in any house since their Bray days. The children seem to have had a happy time playing in the streets on winter evenings. The lanes behind their back garden, close to the canal, included an area called Cott's Cottages and Richmond Parade. These are described nostalgically in 'Araby':

> the dark muddy lanes behind the houses where we ran gauntlet of the rough tribes from the cottages, to the back doors of the dark dripping gardens where odours arose from the ashpits, to the dark odorous stables where a coachman smoothed and combed the horse or shook music from the buckled harness.

Richard Ellmann, Joyce's biographer, says this address received more attention from Joyce than any of the others. Two of the early stories in *Dubliners*, 'An Encounter' and 'Araby', have strong connections with the area. Joyce made use of many of the neighbours; characters from five of the twenty houses on the street appear on the pages of *Dubliners*, *Ulysses* and *Finnegans Wake*. Only fourteen houses now remain.

Across the street from the Joyce home was number one, where the Boardman family lived. Eddy and Eily Boardman feature in the Nausicaa episode of *Ulysses*. In 'Araby' the same house serves as the home of Mangan and his sister: 'Every morning I lay on the floor in the front parlour watching the door. The blind was pulled down within an inch of the sash so that I could not be seen.'

John Clancy, who worked in the sub-sheriff's office, lived in number seven, and appears under his own name in *Finnegans Wake*, and as Long John Fanning in *Ulysses*. Later, he was elected Lord Mayor of Dublin, but died before assuming office. He was caught in a rain-storm on his way home from the City Council meeting that elected him Lord Mayor, and developed pneumonia. The Clancy Chain is now used by the Lord Mayor of Dublin on an everyday basis.

The garden of Dillon's house, number twenty, where Joe and his fat young brother, Leo, lived, provided the venue for the boys in 'An Encounter' to fight their Indian battles. The Mahon brothers lived in number five and the name Mahoney may have been derived from them for the character based on Stanislaus in 'An Encounter'.

From 1 Richmond Parade, Joyce got the character of Lenehan in 'Two Gallants'; while at the other end of the Parade in number six, Cissy Caffrey and the twins, Tommy and Jacky, lived, who appear in *Ulysses* with their neighbour, Eddy Boardman.

Like their Drumcondra home, the Joyces had happy days here also. On Sundays and holidays John Joyce, who had a great knowledge of local lore and history, still went for long walks with his friends, both into the countryside and around the city. Joyce and Stanislaus usually accompanied him. John Joyce loved to point out the various places of historic or literary interest to the group, such as the home of the surgeon, Sir William Wilde, at 1 Merrion Square, or the residence of Francis Higgins, known as Sham Squire, on St Stephen's Green. According to Stanislaus, his father had an inexhaustible fund of Dublin small talk, and Joyce shared with him this interest in Dublin lore, which distance and lapse of time served only to increase.

May Joyce played the piano, and John Joyce sang as he had done in the good old days in Bray when they were all younger and things were better. He sang ballads well, and many operatic airs in English but known by their Italian names, such as 'Ah si, ben mio', 'M'appari', which appears numerous times in *Ulysses*, and many others. Joyce's voice was beginning to develop. He had a beautiful light tenor voice, and he learned a lot about music by listening to his father discuss various singers, as is done in 'The Dead'. He was often invited to sing at Sunday evening parties in the home of David Sheehy, MP, at 2 Belvedere Place adjacent to Fitzgibbon Street. The Sheehy family consisted of two brothers, Richard and Eugene, who went to Belvedere College with Joyce, and four sisters, Margaret, Hanna, Kathleen and Mary,

2 Belvedere Place, home of the Sheehy family.

the youngest, to whom Joyce was attracted for a number of years.

The friendship with this unusual family was the only experience of what might be considered a social life that Joyce and Stanislaus had in Dublin. Joyce was a class ahead of Eugene Sheehy at Belvedere but nevertheless they were close friends. In his book, *May it Please the Court*, Eugene Sheehy described Joyce the schoolboy as aloof, icy and imperturbable. He remembered him then as a tall, slight stripling, with flashing teeth, white as a hound's, pale blue eyes that sometimes had an icy look, and a mobile sensitive mouth. He was fond of throwing back his head as he walked, and his mood alternated between cold, slightly haughty aloofness and sudden boisterous merriment. His sister Mary often thought Joyce was rude, but with her his abrupt manner was a cloak for shyness and affection.

May Joyce often went to the Sheehy's home and played the piano accompaniments to her son's songs. She was very proud and fond of Joyce and he was affectionate to her. Eugene Sheehy rememberd her as a frail, sad-faced and gentle lady whose skill at music suggested a sensitive, artistic temperament. Joyce used to lead her towards the piano with grave, old-world courtesy. Sheehy gave a description of John Joyce as a dapper little man, with military moustache, who sported an eyeglass and cane, and wore spats… to whom Joyce owed his caustic wit. Sheehy also recalled Joyce telling how his father read out an obituary notice of a family friend, Mrs Cassidy, in the *Freeman's Journal* one morning. On hearing the news Mrs Joyce was shocked and cried out: 'Oh! don't tell me that Mrs Cassidy is dead,' to which John Joyce replied, 'Well, I don't quite know about that, but someone has taken the liberty of burying her.'

It was at 13 North Richmond Street that two Dominican priests called to ask John Joyce if he would consider sending Joyce as a boarder, free of charge, to one of their colleges in the country. They were impressed by the results of the Intermediate examinations, in which Joyce had again won an exhibition in the Junior Grade. They were brought into the parlour and Joyce was summoned; his father consulted with him about the proposal put forward, and told him to decide for himself. Joyce said he began with the Jesuits and 'I want to end with them.' He won three exhibitions, and won the prize for English composition twice, in the Middle and Senior Grades. He won a four pound prize for English composition, and Professor Magennis of University College, who read his essay, said that it was publishable. He disliked mathematics and considered it his weakest subject, yet in the Middle Grade he was placed thirteenth in Ireland. He had the ability to grasp a subject at short notice and retain it until the examination was completed. As well as being diligent about his schoolwork, he read widely outside the prescribed school course. He borrowed numerous books from Capel Street Public Library, which was about a mile from his home. This is where he sent Stanislaus for *Jude the Obscure* by Thomas Hardy and Stanislaus, unable to read his writing, had asked the surprised librarian for *Jude the Obscene*, which amused his brother greatly.

During his years attending Belvedere there was a period of three full years when the family did not move residence. The results of the Intermediate examinations, in June 1895, showed that he won an exhibition worth twenty pounds tenable over three years; in December of the same year he was received into the Sodality of the Blessed Virgin Mary and the following September when he was aged fourteen and a half, he was made Prefect of the Sodality. In *A Portrait*, when Stephen is Prefect, the Sodality meets on Saturday mornings in the chapel to recite the office of the Blessed Virgin Mary: 'his place was a cushioned kneeling-desk at the right of the altar from which he led his wing of the boys through the responses.' In June 1897 Joyce won an exhibition worth thirty pounds and the following December during his final year at Belvedere, he was re-elected Prefect of the Sodality. In May of the following year, he played the part of Dr Grimstone in an adaptation of F. Anstey's play *Vice Versa*. Two of his schoolmates dared him to take off the rector during the play, which he did superbly, much to the amusement of Father Henry who was sitting in the front row.

Before Joyce entered University College in the autumn of 1898, the family moved from 13 North Richmond Street. All the house-moving had been noticed by his fellow pupils; often a schoolmate named Fallon asked Joyce with a silly laugh in his voice, 'Why are we on the move again, if it's a fair question?' He did not give the reply that he gave to his sister when she once asked him where their father and mother had gone: 'Becauseboro theboro landboro lordboro putboro usboro outboro.'

III

University Years to
Departure from Ireland,
1898–1904

JOYCE HAD COMPLETED his Senior Grade at Belvedere College in the early summer of 1898. He did not win an exhibition on his results but retained the one he had won the previous year. He entered University College on St Stephen's Green the following autumn, and the family moved once more, back across the River Tolka, to Fairview, a locality in which they remained for the next three years. Fairview is three miles north-east from the city centre and is adjacent to Clontarf, where the famous battle was fought by King Brian Boru on Good Friday 1014, which broke Danish power in Ireland. There are many fine residences on the tree-lined avenues, which branch off the coast road in Clontarf. At Dollymount, which is just beyond Clontarf, the Bull Wall extends one and a half miles south-south-east into Dublin Bay and east of this breakwater is the North Bull Island.

The Joyces moved to 29 Windsor Avenue, Fairview. Stanislaus described it as 'near the road that winds around the shallow mouth of the Liffey to Clontarf. It was the second-last house on the left at the top of parallel rows of two-storey houses bordering on the rather extensive grounds of some invisible suburban villa.' These extensive grounds to which Stanislaus referred have since been covered by a corporation

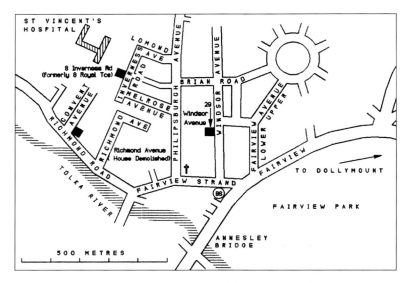

housing estate. The house was owned by a young clergyman called Love, who is incorporated as a character in *Ulysses* by the ever percipient Joyce. It is a small, grey, terraced, two-storey house and is in sharp contrast to the loftiness of the Fitzgibbon Street houses. The original front door has been replaced and there is an side entrance into the back yard.

During the short period they remained in this house, May Joyce gave birth to a still-born male infant, while downstairs John Joyce was assuring a sober friend who had taken him home for the occasion that, 'by God, he's not dead yet'. His last child was already dead. As Stanislaus noted, brief as their stay was in their numerous residences, it was still long enough in most cases to be marked by a death in the family. They remained here until May 1899, and again spent days picnicking and bathing at the nearby Bull Wall and at Howth. The children could walk to their seaside destination from the Dollymount tram terminus. Joyce, being a good walker, used to walk to the Bull Wall and back, a journey of four miles. He is remembered by William Fallon, one of his schoolmates, as being an expert swimmer. This was due in some measure to his lean frame and lithe build, but mainly to his determination to practice. The Bull Wall and Dollymount also appear in *A Portrait* when Stephen passes a group of Christian Brothers as he crosses the wooden bridge on the Bull Wall. Later, he encounters a young fair-haired girl, wading in the water with her skirts drawn up and dovetailed behind her. Her beauty affects him and her image passes

29 Windsor Avenue, Fairview.

into his soul forever: 'On and on and on he strode, far out over the sands, singing wildly to the sea, crying to greet the advent of the life that had cried to him.' A similar incident happened to Joyce about this time, and was to be a turning point in his life.

Joyce read an enormous amount and it was at 29 Windsor Avenue that he first encountered the work of the Norwegian playwright Henrik Ibsen, for whom he had a great admiration. A breath of current European thought entered the Joyce household. Stanislaus recalled the day when a slim volume, in yellow paper covers, containing Ibsen's *The Master Builder* arrived from Heinemann, the publishers. His brother read it into the early hours of the morning. Stanislaus thought it little short of a miracle that anyone should have written or even read poetry while living in that household, typical as it was of the squalor created by a drunken parent.

Early morning in term time, Joyce used to walk the three miles from his home to the university on St Stephen's Green: 'The trees in Stephen's Green were fragrant of rain and the rain-sodden earth gave forth its mortal odour, a faint incense rising upward through the mould from many hearts.' This is how Joyce chronicled the approach of Stephen Dedalus to the 'sombre' college. On his way, Joyce would have cut across St Stephen's Green and out through the little gate of the park onto 'the footpath inside the chains where Stephen had so often walked at night with his friends.' These chains were later used to make armaments for the First World War.

In 1738 the biblically named Abel Ram from Gorey, who was involved in the early development of the Green, owned three building lots, one of which he sold to Hugh Montgomery from County Fermanagh. This was plot number twelve of the 1664 allotment, and the site on which 85 St Stephen's Green was built. The architect was the distinguished Richard Cassels, who had come to Ireland from Saxony in 1727.

Montgomery died in 1739 and the house then passed to George

University College, St Stephen's Green, which Joyce attended from 1898 to 1902.

Johnston. Subsequent owners included Richard Chapel Whaley from Whaley Abbey near Ballinaclash, County Wicklow, who made his fortune from a nearby copper mine. On the proceeds of this he lived in 'fine splendour and prince-like magnificence'. Whaley was living in number eighty-five when he had the adjoining number eighty-six built. It was probably erected around 1765–6, as that date is inscribed on a stone over the fireplace in what was once the kitchen; and 1766 is on a hopper-head that is perched over a door leading into the back garden. With the exception of Iveagh House, these are the only stone-faced houses on St Stephen's Green.

The later occupants of number eighty-five included Lady Bangor; the Clanwilliams (it was long known as Clanwilliam House); George La Touche, whose coat-of-arms can be seen on the stairway; Anthony Blake, and its last private owner, Nicholas Ball, the son of a silkmercer who took his place as Justice of the Common Pleas in 1839 and lived in the house until his death in 1865. It was then sold to the Catholic University.

Cardinal John Henry Newman founded the Catholic University in 1857. The two houses numbers eighty-five and eighty-six, later known as Newman House, were combined in 1854 as St Patrick's House. The Catholic University of Ireland was opened with John Henry Newman as its first Rector. The resident students were accommodated in bedrooms on the two top floors of number eighty-six, which were approached by a separate staircase. Newman had the ground and first floors fitted for the schools of philosophy and letters, while the library was installed in the back drawing-room. The basements of both houses were later joined and remodelled. A new dining area was made, comprising the old refectory and the original Whaley kitchen. When the National University was established and Earlsfort Terrace came into use, Newman House fell into disrepair but was later restored and used by the University. It is now open to the public.

Writing of number eighty-six, a nineteenth-century auctioneer refered 'to the grandeur of the wide Portland stone staircase and the sumptuous stucco decoration of the splendid arched ceilings, in itself an object of great interest, pronounced by the elite of the country as a masterpiece of art'.

The plasterwork differs in each house. Robert West was responsible for number eighty-six, and the Francini brothers for number eighty-five. This feature in both houses makes them period show-pieces. Among the rooms of greatest interest are the salon on the first floor of number eighty-five, and a small back drawing-room in number eighty-six, which overlooks the gardens where the chimney piece of Sienna marble is noteworthy, with the jambs and frieze inlaid.

Number eighty-six is lavishly decorated in rococo style. It is perhaps the last house decorated in this manner before the arrival of the Adam style.

In the early days, the distinguished staff members of the Catholic University included poets Aubrey de Vere and Denis Florence McCarthy; Eugene O'Curry, an expert on Irish manuscript material, and Thomas

Arnold, a professor in the Department of English, and a brother of the poet Matthew Arnold. John Casey, described as 'a man of simple faith and subtle mathematics', taught conics with the help of a raw potato in the old physics theatre.

A plaque was unveiled in 1974 outside Newman House, commemorating three of the most prominent people associated with the university: John Henry Newman, Gerard Manley Hopkins and James Joyce. Just opposite, in St Stephen's Green, is a bust of Joyce by the sculptor Marjorie FitzGibbon. The inscription reads ' "Crossing St Stephens, that is my Green." Erected in 1982 for the centenary of James Joyce's birth.'

During Joyce's first year at university, while he was living at 29 Windsor Terrace, he studied Latin, French, English, Mathematics and Philosophy. He took courses in English from Professor Thomas Arnold, Father George O'Neill,SJ, and Father Joseph Darlington, SJ, who appears in *A Portrait* as the Dean of Studies, who lights the fire and speaks with Stephen Dedalus.

Joyce drew characters for his books from his days at university just as he had done with Clongowes Wood and Belvedere College. As Richard Ellmann points out in his biography of Joyce, the students at University College were more unusual then their professors. Three of Joyce's close friends were to meet violent deaths. Francis Sheehy Skeffington, who appears as McCann in *A Portrait*, was out in the streets attempting to stop the looting during the 1916 Rising, when he was arrested. He was taken to Portobello Barracks where he was shot, without trial, by a British officer who at a subsequent inquiry was found to be insane. Skeffington, a writer and pacifist, had been auditor of the Literary and Historical Society at University College. He was registrar at the University from 1902–04 when he resigned, following a dispute with the President on an issue concerning the rights of women to academic status. He married Hanna Sheehy, the daughter of David Sheehy, MP and assumed her name upon marriage. Skeffington is described in *A Portrait* as 'a squat figure in a shooting jacket and breeches and with a fair goatee'. Another friend was Thomas Kettle, economist, author, one-time auditor of the Literary and Historical Society and editor of *St Stephen's* magazine. Following Skeffington's death, he volunteered for active service with the Royal Dublin Fusiliers and was sent to the Western Front, where he was killed in Givenchy, France, during the Battle of the Somme. Kettle was regarded as one of the most brilliant men of his generation. He is commemorated in St Stephen's Green with a bust.

George Clancy (Davin in *A Portrait*) was an athletic Limerick man and an enthusiast of the Irish language. Under his influence Joyce spent some time learning Irish from Patrick Pearse, who taught members of a branch of the Gaelic League at University College. While Mayor of Limerick, Clancy was murdered in his home by the Black and Tans in full view of his family. Perhaps the closest friend Joyce had was J.F. Byrne who appears in *A Portrait* as the kind and patient Cranly:

> It was a priest-like face, priest-like in its pallor, in the wide winged nose, in the shadowings below the eyes and along the jaws, priest-like in the lips that were long and bloodless and faintly smiling; and Stephen, remembering swiftly how he had told Cranly of all the tumults and unrest and longings in his soul, day after day and night by night, only to be answered by his friend's listening silence, would have told himself that it was the face of a guilty priest who heard confessions of those whom he had not power to absolve but that he felt again in memory the gaze of its dark womanish eyes.

When Joyce entered university he naturally became friendly with Byrne, as he had known him at Belvedere. During their long walks through the streets of Dublin they had lengthy discussions. One chilly December morning Byrne arrived into university a little early for his first class. It was even colder in the building than it had been outside.

The fire in the grate had been lit, but had gone out. Father Darlington arrived, tore up a few *Evening Telegraphs* and duly put them on the grate with some charred pieces of coal on top. He then got three candle-ends, which he placed strategically amid the coals on top of the fire,

7 Eccles Street, home of J.F. Byrne and one of the most famous addresses in literature as the home of Leopold and Molly Bloom.

one on each side and one in the middle. When eventually the fire started
to light, Father Darlington was thoroughly pleased with himself and
his achievement and said to Byrne "'Pon my word Mister – Mister
Byrne, there's quite an art in lighting a fire, is there not!' Byrne related
this incident of Father Darlington and the fire to Joyce who uses it in
A Portrait when the Dean of Studies and Professor of English, Father
Butt, SJ, does the same thing:

> He opened the door of the theatre and halted in the chilly
> grey light that struggled through the dusty windows. A figure
> was crouching before the large grate and by its leanness and
> greyness he knew it was the dean of studies lighting the fire.
> Stephen closed the door quietly and approached the fireplace.
> —Good morning, sir! Can I help you?
> The priest looked up quickly and said:
> —One moment now, Mr Dedalus, as you will see. There is
> an art in lighting a fire… He produced four candle-butts
> from the side-pockets of his soutane and placed them deftly
> among the coals and twisted papers.

On account of his enthusiasm for chess, which Joyce did not share
with him, Byrne was referred to as the 'White Bishop'. Byrne, in his
memoirs entitled *Silent Years*, wrote about his interest in the game.
Joyce used to sit and wait for him for hours on end in the smoke-room
of the D.B.C. coffee shop in Dame Street, while Byrne was playing
chess with John Howard Parnell, the City Marshall and brother of
Charles Stewart Parnell.

In October 1898, after one such game, Joyce conferred the name of
'Cranly' on Byrne, and asked him if he knew where he got it:

> Yes, I do. Since you came to University College last month
> you have heard me occasionally referred to as the 'White

Bishop'. And in the past few weeks there have been a couple of notices about a White Bishop who came here as Archbishop of Dublin five hundred years ago this very month of October. The other night I saw you reading about him in John D'Al-ton's book, the *Memoirs of the Archbishops of Dublin.*

In May 1899, just as Joyce was completing his first year at University, the family were on the move again, though they did not move very far; this time they moved to share a house as lodgers with another family named Hughes in the nearby Convent Avenue. The avenue, which led to the main entrance of St Vincent's Lunatic Asylum, had only three houses on it. In all probability the house that the Joyces lived in was the large end house on the corner of Richmond Road. This could accommodate the two families, consisting of the three in the Hughes family and the twelve Joyces. Hughes, an Ulsterman, was as improvident as John Joyce, and in only a matter of months, the landlord decided to put an abrupt end to the house-sharing enterprise.

In the latter part of 1899, when Joyce was in his second year at University, the family moved again, and had a portion of a larger house (now demolished) at 13 Richmond Avenue, also in Fairview. On 20 January 1900 Joyce read a paper titled, 'Drama and Life' to the Literary and Historical Society, which had been founded by Cardinal Newman and met at the University College at 86 St Stephen's Green. The paper, which concerned Henrik Ibsen, had to be submitted for approval to the Reverend President of the college, who put a blue pencil through some of the passages but, in the end, Joyce won out and read the paper in its entirety. Shortly after the publication of Ibsen's play *When We Dead Awaken*, Joyce astounded all his friends at university by having an article entitled 'Ibsen's New Drama' accepted in the prestigious *Fortnightly Review.* William Archer, a London drama critic, who translated Ibsen's work, relayed a message to Joyce on 23 April 1900, to say that he wished to pass on the author's thanks. In turn, Joyce wrote to

Convent Avenue, where the Joyces shared a house with the Hughes family.

Archer thanking him for his kindness in writing to him and informed him that he was a young Irishman, aged eighteen, who would keep the words of Ibsen in his heart all his life. He received the sum of twelve guineas for the article, which was quite a sum at that time.

The month of May 1900 was a particularly busy one for the Joyces. With his earnings, Joyce brought his father on a trip to London with him. As Stanislaus remarked, his father was always in high spirits at the prospect of amusing himself and squandering a little windfall. They stayed in a cheap boarding house and spent the evenings entertaining themselves at the theatre and the music halls, enjoying Eleanora Duse in *La Citta Morta* and *La Gioconda.* During the visit Joyce looked for a job. With his father, he called on T.P. O'Connor, a politician and journalist who supported Parnell who ran a literary penny journal called *T. P.'s Weekly.* Joyce was interested in journalistic work, but O'Connor was not prepared to employ him as he considered him too young. Joyce then visited W.L. Courtney, the editor of the *Fortnightly Review.* He called on William Archer, who took him to lunch. Archer was the first literary person to take any real notice of him. Father and son returned home in great spirits with twopence change between them.

In the same month as Joyce was completing his second year at university, the family rented a fine house at 8 Royal Terrace, Fairview, subsequently called Inverness Road. They always moved with great intentions, but according to Stanislaus, each succeeding house had an emptier look. The main reason for all the moving was that John Joyce would not pay the rent: 'To demand money for eatables seemed to him just, but to expect people to pay for shelter the exorbitant sums which are demanded annually by houseowners in Dublin seemed to him unjust.'

Royal Terrace is still much the same as when the Joyces lived there. The terrace adjoins a number of neat little roads with such names as Waverley, Melrose and Lomond. These names are a reminder that the area was once a Scottish colony, accommodating families connected with the Dublin Distillers Company, nearby on the banks of the Tolka. Stanislaus recounted that some of his happiest recollections were associated with Royal Terrace such as accompanying his younger brother, George, swimming on a hazy summer day, or trespassing in somebody's park in which there was a little lake.

This grey, cement-faced house in Royal Terrace has two-storeys over a basement with steps leading up to the front door. It has a sunken front garden, surrounded by railings. The Joyce children explored the back garden when they first arrived at their new home and found two books at the end of the garden which they called the ashpit books.

8 Royal Terrace, Fairview.

The back lane where Stephen Dedalus, in A Portrait, *hears the screeches of a mad nun. The convent is on the far side of the wall on the right.*

One was a Protestant Bible and the other a songbook. Overlooking St Vincent's Hospital, the garden is much the same, affording room for a clothes line and a few bins with a door leading on to a back lane. This narrow, curving lane behind the houses is just as it was in *A Portrait*. In the book, Stephen slips out the back gate into the lane behind the house, to avoid the rancour of his father: 'The lane behind the terrace was waterlogged and as he went down it slowly, choosing his steps amid the heaps of wet rubbish he heard a mad nun screeching in the nuns' madhouse beyond the wall. – Jesus Jesus, Jesus!' On his long morning walk to the University, Stephen Dedalus would pass the sloblands of Fairview. This area has been reclaimed and now forms Fairview Park. Sometimes he would take the tram as far as Amiens Street Station where he would alight 'because he wished to partake of the morning life of the city'.

In the summer of 1900 John Joyce was employed in the midland town of Mullingar to revise the election list. He went there accompanied by Joyce and other members of the family. *Stephen Hero* contains a section about their time in Mullingar. Stephen departs from Broadstone Railway Station in Dublin which was the terminus for passenger traffic on the Midlands and Great Western Railway. On the fifty-mile journey, he is cramped in a third class carriage between some unwashed labourers, each of whom has a little bundle tied in a spotted handkerchief. In the novel the events are altered considerably, such as Stephen staying with Mr Fuller, his godfather. Philip McCann, who died in 1898, was Joyce's' godfather and had no connection with Mullingar.

During his stay in the town, Joyce translated two of Hauptmann's plays, *Vor Sonnenaufgang (Before Sunrise)* and *Michael Kramer*. As usual, he observed his surroundings and years later chose Phil Shaw's photographic shop in Earl Street as the place of employment for Leopold Bloom's fifteen-year-old daughter Milly in *Ulysses*. Her father thought she would be better off in Mullingar than in Dublin, 'riding Harry Devan's bike at night in Nelson Street, and smoking cigarettes in the skating rink.' When in the 'Hades' episode Paddy Dignam's funeral cortege is passing over the Royal Canal at Crossguns Bridge in Dublin, Bloom considers visiting Milly 'by canal, or cycle down'.

During this period in Mullingar Joyce made notes for *Stephen Hero* and wrote his first play, *A Brilliant Career*. According to Stanislaus, it was completed by July 1900. It concerns a young doctor who jilts his first love to marry a woman who can further his career. Eventually he is made mayor of the town. Due to a bad sewage system a plague breaks out and, in curbing the outbreak, he is helped by the woman whom he had betrayed. The play ends on a bitter note with the breaking up of the mayor's marriage. On his return to Dublin Joyce posted the manuscript of the play to William Archer and had a reply by 15 August informing him that he had talent, possibly more than talent, but that the play was not wholly successful. Archer assured him that he'd be interested in receiving further dramatic material from him.

In the autumn of 1900 Joyce started his third year at university taking Latin, French, English, Italian and Logic as subjects. Like the majority of students at the University College, he studied mostly in the National Library in Kildare Street, a fine well proportioned neo-Palladian edifice built in 1885–90. Joyce had used the library from the time he finished at Belvedere right through his university days and after. He generally read there until it closed in the evening at ten o'clock: 'Stephen repaired to the Library where he was supposed to be engaged in serious work. As a matter of fact he read little or nothing in the Library. He talked with Cranly by the hour either at a table, or, if removed by the librarian or by the indignant glances of the students, standing at the top of the staircase.' J.F. Byrne recalled that Joyce was ordered to leave the reading room by the librarian, Thomas Lyster, on account of sending a howl of laughter through it. He was convulsed at the title of a book that Byrne was reading, *Diseases of the Ox*. Byrne tried to explain to Lyster, but Lyster snapped, 'Yes, Mr Byrne, I know, but Mr Joyce should learn to control himself, and I must ask him to leave the reading room, and to stay out of it, until he does.' Joyce struggled to his feet, and Byrne stood up to join him. 'I don't mean you, Mr Byrne. Of course you can stay.' Byrne explained that he would have to help Joyce out as he would never make it as far as the turnstile on his own. Byrne had farming friends in Wicklow who had a query concerning one of their cows, and Byrne asked the assistance of Lyster in looking up a book that might help him solve the problem with the cow. In *A Port-rait*, Joyce writes of 'Stephen pointing to the title page of Cranly's book on which was written ' " Diseases of the Ox".'

It was from 8 Royal Terrace that Joyce, in March 1901, wrote his famous letter to Ibsen to greet him on his seventy-third birthday.

The Joyce family remained in Royal Terrace until late 1901, when John Joyce moved his entourage to 32 Glengariff Parade, off the North Circular Road. As before, it was probably a case of non-payment of rent that prompted the move. Through years of experience, John Joyce was becoming an expert at handling his various landlords. When they wished to evict him and his family, John Joyce would persuade them that there was no way he could find alternative accommodation without showing his prospective landlord receipts of rent paid for the previous few months. This ploy worked; the exasperated landlord would provide these in order to have his premises vacated and avoid legal costs.

Initially, it took two large vans to remove all the furniture. With each subsequent move various bits and pieces of furniture had been sold off, and by the time they were moving from Royal Terrace to Glengariff Parade, only one float was required. In this instance, Stanislaus remembered that towards evening some of the family had gone ahead to the new house and, as the last of them left Royal Terrace and walked slowly after the float, with the dray-horse straining under the weight, John Joyce kept lilting one of his songs to himself. He was pleased that his trick with the landlord had worked again. One thing to which he attached great importance during the migrations was the careful transportation of the family portraits. He regarded these as his credentials and they had to be carried by hand.

10 Glengariff Parade (formerly 32 Glengariff Parade).

Glengariff Parade was described by Stanislaus as a depressing neighbourhood. It has the high walls of Mountjoy Jail, which was built in 1850, as a backdrop. This redbrick terrace house, 32 Glengariff Parade, renumbered 10 in 1952, is the third house on the terrace on the left-hand side after the small laneway coming from the direction of the North Circular Road. It has a bow window looking onto the street and a small neat back garden overlooked by the grey prison wall. The accommodation then consisted of two bedrooms with a living-room and kitchen. As in North Richmond Street, the Royal Canal is about a hundred yards from the house.

Towards the end of the summer in 1901 Joyce assembled a collection of his poems and composed musical settings for them. He wrote to William Archer, having read that he was preparing a book on young poets. Archer wrote an honest criticism on the poems, saying he preferred poetry embodying a definite thought or a distant picture, rather than poetry which suggests only a mood. Joyce started making notes of what he termed epiphanies, ironical observations of slips and little errors and gestures by which people betrayed their secrets. In the autumn of 1901 he entered his final year at University College taking English, French and Italian as his degree subjects. In October he wrote a short article on the proposed National Theatre for the college magazine, *St Stephen's*, entitled 'The Day of the Rabblement' which was rejected. Skeffington had also had an article, advocating equal status for women at the university entitled 'A Forgotten Aspect of the Univeristy Question' rejected by the same censor. On the suggestion of Joyce, they decided to have the essays printed as a pamphlet at their own expense. They had eighty-five copies printed by Gerrard Brothers at St Stephen's Green priced at two pence. The publication of the essays aroused great interest among students of the university and Joyce's article provoked much discussion. It started with a quotation: 'No man, said the Nolan, can be a lover of the true or the good unless he abhors the multitude; and the artist, though he may employ the crowd, is very careful to isolate himself.' No one had any idea who the Nolan was, and Stanislaus urged his brother to enlighten them that it was Giordano Bruno of Nola, but Joyce retorted, 'Laymen should be en-couraged to think.' Some comments were published in *St Stephen's* about the pamphlet. In one, the reviewer wrote that Joyce was 'corrupted, as we do verily believe, by the learning of Italie or othere foreigne parts, hath no care for Holye Religion, but is fain to mislead our players.' The editor, Hugh Kennedy, wrote, 'If Mr Joyce thinks that the artist must stand apart from the multitude, and means he must also sever himself from the moral and religious teachings which have, under Divine guidance, moulded its spiritual character, we join issue with him, and we prophesy but ill-success for any school which offers the Irish public art based upon such a principle.'

On 15 February 1902 Joyce read another paper to the Literary and Historical Society, this time on James Clarence Mangan. The *Freeman's Journal* reported the meeting the following day: 'James Joyce was deservedly applauded at the conclusion of what was generally agreed to have been the best paper ever read before the Society.'

In early 1902 the months approaching his degree examinations were difficult for Joyce due to the family circumstances and the illness of his young brother George, who was suffering from typhoid fever. George was a handsome, gifted boy to whom his mother was deeply attached. When she took him walking on the esplanade in Bray, he attracted the attention of passers-by with his good looks and golden hair. He was a pupil at Belvedere College where he mastered Latin with little apparent effort, in circumstances where study was difficult at the best of times.

During his illness, May Joyce was undecided about whether she should take him to the nearby Mater Misericordiae Hospital or nurse him at home. She kept him at home and nursed him through many weeks until the doctor said that he was out of danger and informed her that she could give her son, 'soup, meat, anything you like'. What followed was harrowing for all the family but especially for his mother. Against her better judgment, she gave George some food that proved fatal. Stanislaus was sent running for a doctor and someone else for the priest while George said to his terrified mother, 'I am very young to die.' During his illness, Stanislaus, when he came back from school, read 'The Bottle Imp' to him and Joyce played the piano in the parlour and sang for him, leaving the doors open so that George could hear him from his bed. He died of peritonitis on 9 March 1902.

Two Jesuit teachers from Belvedere came to offer their condolences and Father Tomkin, the rector of the college, arranged for him to have a public funeral from the college chapel. According to Stanislaus, John Joyce did not feel his son's death very deeply, but his mother never recovered from it; she could not forgive herself for having obeyed the doctor's instructions. When Stanislaus returned to school after the funeral he felt raw and restless. He was two-and-half-years older than George and they had been close companions. Another brother, Charlie, who was a year older than George, and who had paired off with him as children do in large families, entered the seminary in Clonliffe Road in 'his dumb sorrow and loneliness'.

George's death affected Joyce deeply and he records his illness in *Stephen Hero*, with Isabel, Stephen's sister, substituted for George:

> She showed very little animation except when the piano was playing in the room below and then she made them leave the bedroom door open and closed her eyes. Money was still scarce and still the doctor ordered delicacies... the doctor came with Mr Dedalus on a car, examined the girl and asked

had she seen a priest. He went away saying that while there was life there was hope but she was very low: he would call in the morning. Isabel died a little after midnight. Her father, who was not quite sober walked about the room on tiptoe, cried in little fits every time his daughter showed a change and kept on saying 'That's right, duckey: take that now' whenever her mother forced her to swallow a little champagne and then nodded his head until he began to cry afresh.

One of Joyce's epiphanies suggests how close he was to his brother:

They are all asleep. I will go now… He lies on my bed where I lay last night! They have covered him with a sheet and closed his eyes with pennies… Poor little fellow! We have often laughed together. He bore his body very lightly… I am very sorry he died. I cannot pray for him as the others do. Poor little fellow! Everything is so uncertain!

Afterwards, Stanislaus often found his mother in the kitchen or sitting alone sewing the children's clothes with tears streaming down her face. The death of George devastated her.

In May 1902 *St Stephen's* published the paper on Mangan that Joyce had read to the Literary and Historical Society. His arts degree completed, he decided to embark upon a medical career with his friend J.F. Byrne and registered for a course in St Cecilia's medical school in Dublin. This was short-lived due to financial reasons.

On 24 October John Joyce, fondly believing his children were approaching independence, decided to commute half of his pension and invest in 7 St Peter's Terrace, Phibsborough, one in a row of red-brick houses. In 1905, 7 St Peter's Terrace was renumbered and it is now 5 St Peter's Road. Stanislaus thought that the move was perhaps precipitated by his father's transient twinges of conscience, after George's

The BA degree class of 1902 in the garden of University College. Front row: *Felix Hackett, Seumas O'Kelly, Michael Lennon, C.P. Curran.* Middle row: *G. George Clancy, the Revd E. Hogan, SJ, Professor Edouard Cadic, the Revd Joseph Darlington, SJ.* Back row: *the Revd George O'Neill, SJ, James Joyce, J.M. O'Sullivan, R.J. Kinahan, James Clandillon, Patrick Semple.*

death. The house consists of two reception rooms, a kitchen, three bedrooms and a small garden at the back. The original door has been replaced. John Joyce then had the meagre monthly sum of £5 10s 1d. to support six daughters and three sons. He descended rapidly into financial disaster and this led Stanislaus to call their abode 'the house of the bare table'.

On 31 October the degree of Bachelor of Arts was conferred on Joyce, who then decided to leave Ireland. He wrote to Lady Gregory informing her of his plans to study medicine in Paris and asked for her assistance. She wrote to W.B. Yeats in London. On 1 December 1902 Joyce departed from Dun Laoghaire. He was met *en route* by Yeats at Euston Station. Yeats spent the day with him and gave him a number of literary introductions to people whom he thought might prove useful.

St Peter's Road, Phibsborough, of which St Peter's Terrace formed a part.

On arrival in Paris, Joyce settled in at a hotel in the rue Corneille. He attended a few medical lectures but soon gave these up; he then lived the life of a bohemian student and wrote a number of reviews for the *Daily Express*. His father took out a mortgage on the house to enable him to return home for the Christmas break. He stayed for almost a month, and visited the Sheehys and the National Library, where he met the witty medical student Oliver St John Gogarty for the first time. A conversation at the counter of the Library was the start of their friendship.

Joyce returned to Paris on 23 January 1903. At this time he met J.M. Synge, who showed him the manuscript of his play *Riders to the Sea*. He wrote often to his mother, not to comfort her but to complain bitterly of his lack of money and food. She pawned whatever things she had to send him money orders for a few shillings. Her own health was deteriorating and on 10 April Joyce received a telegram: MOTHER DYING. COME HOME. FATHER. He borrowed money from one of his pupils to pay his fare home. The doctors diagnosed that she had cirrhosis of the liver. She improved slightly and was able to get out of her bed for a few hours each afternoon. At Easter, she begged Joyce to make his Easter duty but he refused, just as Stephen recalls in *Ulysses*. In *A Portrait*, Stephen tells Cranly that he had an unpleasant quarrel with his mother about religion.

> She wishes me to make my Easter duty.
> —And will you?
> —I will not, Stephen said.
> —Why not? Cranly said.
> —I will not serve, answered Stephen.

As the summer wore on her condition gradually deteriorated. Joyce wandered aimlessly about without the will to work or do book reviews. He met George Russell at intervals who praised his poems.

It was Joyce's favourite aunt, Josephine Murray, who devoted her time to nursing May Joyce in her last illness. Joyce sang for her, just as he had done for his brother George when he was dying. As May

Joyce's health deteriorated so John Joyce's drinking increased. One day, to the horror of all present, he staggered into her room and blurted out, 'I'm finished. I can't do any more. If you can't get well, die. Die and be damned to you!' Stanislaus attacked his father, calling him a swine, while his mother tried to get out of bed to separate them. Joyce led his father out to another room while May tried to pacify Stanislaus by saying, 'You mustn't do that. You must promise me never to do that, you know that when he is that way he doesn't know what he is saying.'

May Joyce died at home, of cancer on 13 August 1903, aged forty-four, surrounded by her family and her eldest brother John Murray. According to Stanislaus the behaviour of his father hastened her death. She was buried in Glasnevin cemetery where her husband wept inconsolably, 'I'll soon be stretched beside her. Let him take me whenever he likes.' In fact, he lived on until 1931. Stanislaus was enraged by these hypocritical whinings and upbraided his father, who contented himself with saying, ' You don't understand, boy.' Joyce tried to console his ten-year-old sister, Mabel, who was sitting weeping on the stairs of St Peter's Terrace: 'You mustn't cry like that, there's no reason to cry. Mother's in Heaven. She's far happier now than she's ever been on earth but if she sees you crying it'll spoil her happiness. You must remember that when you feel like crying. You can pray for her, if you wish. Mother would like that. But you mustn't cry anymore.'

Joyce dallied for a while in Dublin, unsuccessfully applying for a post in the National Library. Professor Edward Dowden of Trinity College, to whom he went seeking support for the post, found him 'extraordinary' and 'quite unsuitable'. In January 1904 he wrote a short story titled 'A Portrait of an Artist', which he submitted to John Eglinton, editor of the literary magazine *Dana*. It was rejected, and Joyce recast and expanded it into *Stephen Hero*. This in turn was rejected by a publisher and Joyce, in a fit of despair, attempted to destroy the manuscript. Later he rewrote it and in its changed, polished form it was published in 1916 as *A Portrait of the Artist as a Young Man*.

In 7 St Peter's Terrace most of the furniture had been pawned and what remained was broken. When John Joyce took out the last mortgage on the premises he was left with nothing of the nine hundred pounds he had got the previous year by commuting his pension. Worse again, he sold the piano, which roused Joyce to fury. Stanislaus kept a diary around this time that gives us an insight into the disorder of the household. The patient and kind May Joyce had kept the house together at the cost of her life and after her death it fell into complete disarray.

John Joyce was left with three sons and six daughters, ranging in age from twenty-one to ten. For many years he regarded his family as an encumbrance of which he was anxious to rid himself at the earliest opportunity. When there was any money in the house it was impossible to do anything because of his drunkenness and quarrelsome nature, and when there was no money it was equally impossible to do anything because of the hunger and cold and lack of light. Joyce, Stanislaus and Charles never went out on the same night because they did not wish to leave their sisters on their own with their father, as he could lose his temper and fling something at them. He had an abusive and insulting tongue and addressed his children in a scurrilous fashion as 'wastrels' and 'little bastards'.

The eldest daughter, Margaret, known as 'Poppie', now aged twenty, took over the running of the household and her greatest difficulty was to get money from her father when he drew his pension on the twenty-seventh day of each month. For the most part, all she got was abuse. However, within two years the family had scattered.

As far as Joyce was concerned, 7 St Peter's Terrace had ceased to be his home. In late March 1904 he rented a very large room that spanned the top of 60 Shelbourne Road, Ballsbridge, a modest, well-preserved, early Victorian house in a curved terrace, where a family named McKernan lived. He paid for this with money he had borrowed from Oliver St John Gogarty, J.F. Byrne and from George Russell. The room was large enough to fit a piano, which Joyce duly ordered. He

60 Shelbourne Road, where Joyce rented a room for a few months in 1904.

was out when it arrived to avoid tipping the delivery men who, finding no one in, took the piano back with them.

In April Gogarty wrote to Joyce a number of times inviting him over to Oxford. Joyce could not afford the passage, and wrote to Gogarty asking him if he would have a cricket shirt or decent suit to spare as he was trying to get a singing engagement in the Kingstown Pavilion. Around this time Joyce met the famous Irish tenor John McCormack in the company of Richard Best of the National Library. Best was keenly interested in the Féis Ceoil (Festival of Music) and both he and McCormack encouraged Joyce to enter in 1904. Joyce, who had a high, clear, tenor voice, pawned some of his books for the entrance fee.

The Féis Ceoil took place on 16 May 1904 and Joyce was the last candidate in the competition on a list of twenty names. The two set pieces Joyce sang were 'Come, Ye Children' from Sullivan's *Prodigal Son*, and 'A Long Farewell', which was an Irish air. The adjudicator,

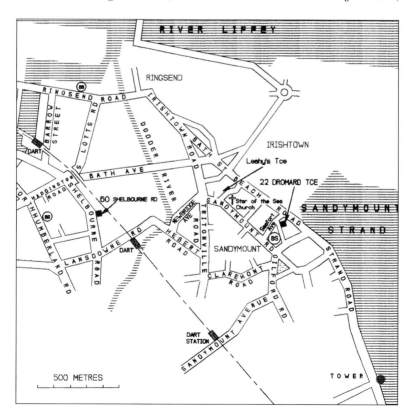

Professor Luigi Denza, intended to award the gold medal to Joyce, but when he was asked to sing a third piece at sight, Joyce refused and strode off the platform, much to Denza's amazement. As a result he was awarded a bronze medal, which, according to Gogarty, he tossed into the Liffey as he was unable to pawn it.

Shortly after this Joyce got a job as a schoolteacher at Clifton School in Summerfield Lodge, Dalkey Avenue, where he remained only until the end of June. It is a fine, substantial house standing in its own grounds and was, at one time, the home of the nineteenth-century poet and critic Denis Florence McCarthy. The founder of the school was Francis Irwin, an Ulster Scot and a graduate of Trinity College. The school is depicted as Mr Deasy's establishment in the Nestor Episode in *Ulysses*, where the headmaster is modelled on Francis Irwin. Joyce uses the names of students he taught there as models for the pupils in *Ulysses*.

On 10 June 1904 his lifelong passion for Nora Barnacle began. Her lasting fame is that she was his model for Molly Bloom in *Ulysses*, Bertha in the play *Exiles*, and Gretta Conroy in the story 'The Dead'.

IV
Nora Barnacle's Galway,
1884–1904

NORA BARNACLE'S parents, Annie Healy and Thomas Barnacle, were married in Galway on 27 January 1881. Thomas Barnacle was thirty-five and was thirteen years older than his wife. For a short period after their marriage, they stayed with Annie's mother, Mrs Catherine Healy, and her brother Thomas at their home in Whitehall. This is an extension of St Augustine Street and is close to the Galway dock area. The couple then took a room in a tenement in Abbeygate Street, which was around the corner from their former address (see map). At the turn of the century many working-class people lived in tenements as few could afford to rent or buy their own home.

Between 1882 and 1896 the Barnacles had eight children: six girls and two boys. All of Annie Healy's children were born at home with the exception of Nora and Kathleen. During this time they had seven different addresses, all within the same close-knit area in the heart of Galway City. Nora, their second child, was born in the maternity section of the Galway Workhouse Hospital on either 21 or 22 March 1884. There is some confusion concerning the date of her birth, as church and state records disagree. The workhouse hospital was a fine stone building situated in the grounds of the present University College Hospital.

Whitehall, Galway, an extension of St Augustine Street, home of Catherine Healy, Nora's grandmother.

During the famine years of 1845–6 the workhouse housed over one-thousand inmates. Originally there was a small hospital for them, but with the fall off in numbers, the workhouse hospital became the city hospital. The fact that Nora was born in hospital and baptized on the same day would indicate that there were complications at her birth. Her name, registered as Norah, was how her mother spelt it; her daughter spelt it similarly until she met Joyce. It then became Nora.

Between the years 1882 and 1896, Nora's parents' addresses included Prospect Hill, near Eyre Square; Raleigh Row, which is behind the Jesuit Church on the old road from Galway to Connemara; Newtownsmyth and finally, in 1899 they settled in a small two-storey artisan's dwelling at 8 Bowling Green (formerly number four), which is near Lynch's Window. The house, built in 1855, consists of one room on the ground floor and another room directly above it; both rooms have timbered ceilings.

The house has not been altered structurally but a cooking range of the period has been installed in the kitchen. There was no water laid on to the house, but a pump, which served all the houses in Bowling Green, was conveniently sited opposite the Barnacle home. Mrs Barnacle lived here until her death in 1939. A plaque indicates that it is the Nora Barnacle House Museum. The house, which was bought by two Galway sisters, Sheila and Mary Gallagher, was renovated and is open to the public during the summer months.

Possibly because of overcrowding, and to ease the burden on her mother, Nora was fostered at an early age by her maternal grandmother,

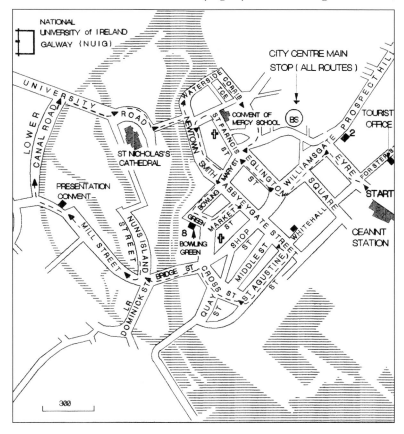

Eyre Square.

Raleigh Row.

Mrs Catherine Healy, who lived in St Augustine Street with her son Thomas. Nora never forgave her mother for shutting her out, although she was much better off materially with Mrs Healy. Her personality and character were formed by Mrs Healy who was kind to her and taught her the correct forms of speech and good table manners. She was better fed and clothed, with her uncle buying her such small luxuries as a pair of buttoned boots.

8 Bowling Green, the home of Nora.

Nora's father, Thomas Barnacle, worked as a baker, as his father had done before him. Joyce gave this description of her parents in a letter to his brother Stanislaus: 'Papa had a shop but drank all the buns and loaves like a man. The mother's family are "toney",' here, he is referring to Patrick and Catherine Mortimer Healy, who had some claim to gentility. Annie Healy had attended the Mercy Convent and was a skilled dressmaker. She had two brothers, Michael and Thomas. Michael was an excellent student and became a successful civil servant, working as Inspector of Customs and Receiver of Wrecks. He was a prominent figure around Galway. Thomas made a good living, working as a handyman.

In 1889, when she was five, Nora started her education at the same school her mother had attended, the local Convent of Mercy National School, Newtownsmyth, just behind Bowling Green. She made her First Communion in St Nicholas' Pro-Cathedral, which is situated at the corner of Middle Street and Abbeygate Street. She remained at the convent until 1897, when she was twelve, having had a free basic education consisting of reading, writing, arithmetic and needlework.

On New Year's day 1897 Mrs Catherine Healy died of bronchitis, aged seventy-six. She was the person to whom Nora was closest and her death was a bitter blow to her. Her uncle, Thomas Healy, then took over as her guardian.

With her striking good looks and thick, auburn hair, Nora attracted admirers from an early age. Her first love was a neighbour from William Street, Michael Feeny, a young schoolteacher whom she had known all her life. A few weeks after her grandmother's death, Michael Feeny died of pneumonia in the City Hospital. He was buried in Rahoon Cemetery, two miles from the city

It was around this time that Nora's mother and father parted. Mrs Barnacle threw her husband out of the house; she had become tired of his drinking, which had cost him his bakery. He was fortunate in being a journey-man baker as he got employment in local bakeries in Galway and also in bakeries as far out as Oughterard.

On leaving school in 1897, Nora got a job in the Presentation Convent. It is interesting to know how she got it; Mrs Barnacle had a neighbour and friend, named Agnes Moloney, whose husband, Martin, had a grocery store in Lombard Street. When he originally set up his shop, his first customers were the Mercy Sisters, but Agnes had even better connections; her sister, Sister Aloysius, was Reverend Mother in the Presentation Convent. Mrs Barnacle asked Agnes if she could find her daughter a job and the Mercy Nuns had recommended Nora to the Moloneys. Agnes then informed Sister Aloysius about Nora, who in turn gave Nora the job as Portress in the convent, where she remained until her departure from Galway in the spring of 1904.

During her girlhood, when she had money saved for sweets, Nora accompanied her friend Mary O'Holleran to Bodkin's shop at 2 Prospect Hill (off Eyre Square). The shop is now an off licence. Bodkin is an old Galway family which was among the 'tribes' of the city. Mr Bodkin had

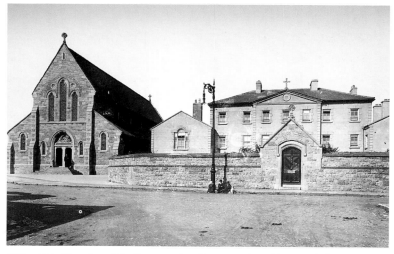

St Joseph's Church and the Presentation Convent, where Nora worked as a portress from 1897 to 1904.

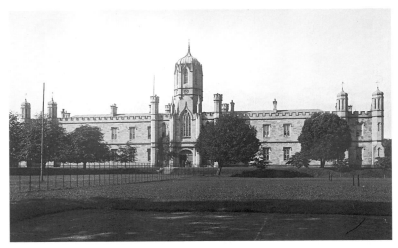

Queen's College, Galway, where Michael Bodkin, one of Nora's admirer's, studied.

a handsome dark-haired son, Michael (Sonny), aged eighteen and a student at University College, Galway (then known as Queen's College). He was an admirer of Nora, and she, in turn, was in love with him. He gave her a present of a bracelet, which she treasured all her life. Michael died of tuberculosis in the County Infirmary before his studies were completed. As with Michael Feeny, he was buried in Rahoon Cemetery. His grave, which consists of a raised stone vault, bears the inscription 'Michael Bodkin, son of Patrick L, and Winifred, died on 11th February 1900 at the age of 20'. A few paces away, in the same cemetery, Nora's father, Thomas Barnacle, lies buried. He died on 13 July 1921.

Joyce, in his story 'The Dead', portrays Nora as Gretta Conroy, and models Michael Furey on Michael Bodkin. However, he used the cemetery in Oughterard as his burial place; Michael Bodkin had no connection with it. Joyce possibly heard Nora speak of her father working in Oughterard as a baker, and liked the musicality of the name. Bodkin appears in Joyce's play *Exiles* and in the poem 'She Weeps over Rahoon', in which Joyce tries to express Nora's thoughts on her past boyfriend.

Michael Bodkin's grave in Rahoon Cemetery.

Nun's Island on the River Corrib, which is part of Galway city, features in 'The Dead' as the location of the house of Gretta's grandmother. Nora's paternal grandmother may have lived here, though there is no evidence that she did. Soon after Michael Bodkin's death, Nora had another admirer. Willie Mulvagh was a Protestant boy with whom she went out walking. He lived in Mary Street. She remarked later that she did not love him, but did it to pass the time. Willie Mulvagh was a bright, intelligent young man who was educated at the Grammar School, situated on College Road. He studied accountancy and worked in the firm of Joe Young, which manufactured mineral water in Eglinton Street. When Thomas Healy learned of the courtship he strongly objected and forbade Nora to meet him again. She continued to see him and arranged secret meetings, on the pretext that she was attending evening devotions in the Abbey Church in Francis Street. But her luck ran out. One evening Thomas Healy saw them out walking together, followed her home and punished her severely with a beating for

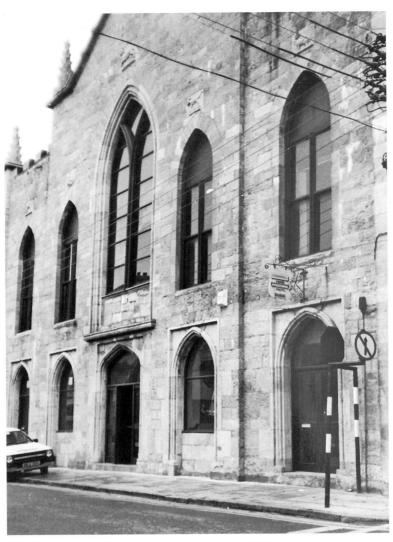

St Nicholas' Pro-Cathedral situated at the corner of Middle and Abbeygate Streets.

disobeying him. (Like Michael Bodkin, Joyce uses Willie Mulvagh in *Ulysses*. He is featured as Mulvey under the Moorish walls in Gibraltar as a lover of the young Molly Bloom.)

The following week, which was sometime in the early months of 1904, with spirited independence, the nineteen-year-old Nora Barnacle stepped on a train bound for Dublin, a place where her uncle would no longer follow her. This was the start of what were to be the nomadic peregrinations of this extraordinary girl from Galway.

Alighting at Broadstone Railway Station, which lies at the junction of the Western Way with Phibsborough Road and Constitution Hill, she made her way to a servant's registry, owned and run by Miss Gardiner, at 15 Leinster Street, which is an extension of Nassau Street. This resulted in her job as a chambermaid in nearby Finn's Hotel. Up to 1899 the premises at 1–2 Leinster Street were operated by Miss E.M. Gardiner as a tea room. In 1900 Mr J.M. Finn, a native of Limerick, opened it as a private hotel and restaurant. He already owned a hotel in Limerick. Finn's Hotel ceased to be a hotel in 1947, and became operated solely as a restaurant. The name is still discernible on the gable end of the building. The hotel contained an elegant stairway

Broadstone Station, Dublin, where Nora Barnacle arrived from Galway in 1904.

Finn's Hotel, Leinster Street, where Nora worked as a chambermaid.

up through its four storeys. On each floor there were four bedrooms and a large suite. The suite was incorporated in a bow-shaped extension to the rear of the main building. These rooms had an uninterrupted view over College Park. Interestingly, as the hotel was built on a curve of the street, one can see from the front upstairs windows as far as

Nora Barnacle.

Mount Street Bridge on the Grand Canal. This view would have incorporated 1 Merrion Square, the former home of Oscar Wilde.

Nora had every alternate evening off work, and took the opportunity of discovering the city.

V
Joyce and Nora:
Exile

JOYCE ALWAYS LIKED to think of Nora as 'sauntering' into his life, and this is precisely what happened. In was summer, 10 June 1904, the twenty-two year old Joyce, dressed in a dark suit, tennis shoes, and sporting a yachting cap and ashplant, was walking down Nassau Street when he caught sight of a tall girl with striking good looks and magnificent auburn hair. She had good carriage and a lively and vibrant air about her. He stopped and spoke to her. With his steel-blue eyes she thought perhaps he might be Swedish. During their conversation, Joyce discovered that she was employed at the nearby Finn's Hotel, that her name was Nora Barnacle and that she hailed from Galway, former stronghold of the Joyce sept. He arranged to meet her on 14 June, outside Sir William Wilde's house at number 1 Merrion Square, just around the corner from Finn's Hotel. Nora failed to turn up, and Joyce returned to his rented accommodation at 60 Shelbourne Road feeling quite dejected. He wrote to her that evening saying that he had looked for a long time at a crop of reddish-brown hair and decided that it was not hers. Might they make another appointment to suit her? Letters posted in the late evening or the early morning were delivered before lunchtime on the following day. He had a reply before nightfall. A further

Nassau Street, Dublin, where Joyce met Nora for the first time.

meeting was arranged for 16 June, and this appointment Nora kept.

They walked together to Ringsend in what turned out to be a windy evening, checkered with intermittent sunshine. Joyce subsequently immortalised the day in *Ulysses* as a tribute to Nora. After this date, they met frequently, walked out together and exchanged many letters. Soon she was writing to him as 'My precious darling', and in a letter dated 8 July 1904, he addressed her as 'Little pouting Nora', and as 'Dear little brownhead'. Yet he was embarrassed to sign himself 'Jim' and for sometime the couple must have addressed each other as Nora and Mr Joyce. On 22 August Joyce invited her to a concert, to hear him sing in the Antient Concert Rooms in North Brunswick Street (now Pearse Street). He warned her that he would be nervous, but Joyce did not

James Joyce, aged twenty-two, in 1904. This photograph was taken in C.P. Curran's garden, 6 Cumberland Row, North Circular Road.

22 Dromard Terrace, Sandymount, where Joyce spent the night of 16 June (see page 124).

1 Merrion Square, where Joyce arranged his first date with Nora. She didn't keep the appointment.

realize that his accompanist on the piano would become so nervous as to quit and leave him, not only to sing, but to play the piano himself as he sang 'Down by the Sally Gardens'. Nora was delighted with his performance. He shared the platform with J.C. Doyle and John

McCormack. In later life she remarked to friends, 'Jim should have stuck to music instead of bothering with writing.' She remarked to Ettore Schmitz, 'I've always told him that he should give up writing and take up singing. To think that he was once on the same platform as John McCormack.' Stanislaus was perturbed about Nora's hold over his brother and Joyce's friend, Vincent Cosgrave, tried to break up their friendship by telling Nora that Joyce's love for her would never last. Cosgrave found Nora, with her roguish humour and happy disposition, attractive, and tried to win her affections, but in her eyes he was no match or rival for Joyce.

One thing the pair had in common was that neither wished to return to their family homes. Nora felt that she had no real ties with Galway. In a letter written at Shelbourne Road on 29 August 1904, Joyce told Nora how he disliked his home which he regarded as a middle-class affair, ruined by his father's spendthrift habits, his mother was slowly killed by years of trouble and by his father's ill-treatment and, in addition, there was a large family with one brother alone capable of understanding him. When he had looked on his mother's face as she lay in her coffin, a face grey and wasted with cancer, he understood that he was looking on the face of a victim and cursed the system which had made her as she was.

Against this background, Joyce found Nora, with her carefree attitude and her combination of innocence and earthiness, a breath of fresh air. Joyce left his room at Shelbourne Road on 31 August as he could not pay the rent and went back to St Peter's Terrace, but only for a day or so. On 1 September he wrote to Nora, telling her that he had got up early to finish a story he was writing but decided to write to her instead. He reminded her that he now had received thirteen letters from her. He asked Nora if she would be prepared to leave Ireland with him, and if she was not under any misapprehension about him.

During the next two weeks Joyce changed his lodgings with increasing rapidity. On 1 September he was at St Peter's Terrace; on 2

September he was staying for a second time with James H. Cousins, the poet and playwright, at 22 Dromard Terrace, Sandymount. He had stayed here on 16 June 1904. The next night he was with a medical student James O'Callaghan. The following two nights he stayed with his Uncle William, at 103 North Strand Road, Fairview. He wrote to Nora from this address enquiring whether her people were wealthy, to see if she would be deprived of any comforts which she would have been accustomed to at home. His uncle, disapproving of his unseemly hours, locked him out of the house. Joyce ended up on 9 September 1904 in the most unusual residence he was ever to occupy, the Martello Tower in Sandycove with Oliver St John Gogarty, and Samuel Chenevix Trench, an Oxford friend of Gogarty's, who had passionately embraced the Irish Revival. The Martello Tower is situated one mile east of Dun Laoghaire, just off the coast road. Joyce stayed here only until the 15 September, a total of six days, though ironically this is the address that has become the most famous. The sturdy granite tower with its eight-foot thick walls, was built in 1804 as a defence against possible Napoleonic invasion. The entrance was ten feet from the ground and since there was no stairway, a ladder had to be used. A large key opened a heavy door that gave on to the living quarters, which consisted of a circular room with a fireplace. Two narrow apertures in the wall provided some light. The lifestyle in the tower was free and easy. All access was cut off by the residents pulling up the ladder behind them.

The tower was let to Gogarty on a quarterly tenancy at eight pounds per annum under an agreement dated 4 June 1904. In his book, *It Isn't This Time of Year At All*, Gogarty recalled how he and Joyce went out to inspect and take possession of the tower:

> Joyce had an uncle who was a clerk in an attorney's office from whom he had probably heard that possession is nine tenths of the law. He was careful to leave some article of his as a symbol before they moved in. The only moveable thing he

The most unusual residence Joyce was to occupy, the Martello Tower in Sandycove.

possessed was a roll of manuscripts, which contained a score or so of poems written in his clear handwriting. Later these were published in a little book he called *Chamber Music*.

They had interesting visitors. Arthur Griffith, journalist and politician, came out occasionally for the weekend and accompanied Gogarty to the Forty-Foot Bathing Place, which is still just below the tower.

William Bulfin in his book *Rambles in Eireann* remarked that he and a friend were going out for a day's cycling in Dublin and Wicklow one Sunday in early autumn:

As we were leaving the suburbs behind us my comrade, who

knew many different types of Irish people said casually that there were two men living in a tower somewhere to the left, who were creating a sensation in the neighbourhood. They had, he said, assumed a hostile attitude towards the conventions of denationalization, and were, thereby, outraging the feelings of the seoinini. He, therefore, suggested that we should pay them a flying visit. There was no necessity to repeat the suggestion, so we turned off to the left at the next crossroads, and were soon climbing a steep ladder which led to the door of the tower. We entered, and found some men of Ireland in possession, with whom we tarried until far on in the morning. One of them had lately returned from a canoeing tour of hundreds of miles through the lakes and rivers and canals of Ireland, another was reading for a Trinity College degree and assiduously wooing the muses, and another was a singer of songs which spring from the deepest currents of life. The returned mariner of the canoe was an Oxford student, whose button-hole was adorned by the badge of the Gaelic League – a most strenuous Nationalist he was, with a patriotism stronger than circumstances, which moved him to pour forth fluent Irish to every Gael he encountered, in accents blent from the characteristic speech of his Alma Mater and the rolling blas of Connacht. The poet was a wayward kind of genius, who talked in a captivating manner, with a keen, grim humour, which cut and pierced through a topic in bright, strong flashes worthy of the rapier of Swift. The other poet listened in silence, and when we went on the roof, he dispos-ed himself restfully to drink in the glory of the morning.

Joyce's departure from the tower was rather dramatic. He regarded himself as having been evicted. Trench (Haines in *Ulysses*) had a nightmare involving a black panther, and screamed. He grabbed a revolver and fired shots into the fireplace. Joyce understandably was frightened. When Trench resumed screaming, Gogarty called out 'leave him to me' and fired at a collection of pans on the shelf over Joyce's bed. Joyce dressed and left in the rain without a word. The scene of the first episode, the Telemachus chapter in *Ulysses* is set in the tower. On Bloomsday 1962 the tower was formally opened as a Joyce Museum by Sylvia Beach from Shakespeare & Co., Paris, who had published the first edition of *Ulysses* in 1922, in a blue cover with white lettering across it; the national colours of Greece, the home of Ulysses. The museum was run by The Joyce Tower Society until 1965 when it was taken over by Dublin and East Tourism and an extension added in 1978. Joyce wrote to Nora on 26 September from St Peter's Terrace: 'I often wonder if you realize thoroughly what you are about to do.' On 8 October he wrote to the poet Seumas O'Sullivan (James Starkey) asking him to put certain items, including the manuscript of his verses, into his trunk, which he said would be collected from the tower the next day. On 16 September he wrote to Nora from 103 North Strand, Fairview saying, 'there is no life here – no naturalness or honesty. People live to-gether in the same houses all their lives and at the end are as far apart as ever.'

Opposed to marriage, and not wishing to live openly with Nora in Dublin, where he would be unable to support her on his literary earnings, he applied for a job in the Berlitz School in Zurich. On 8 October they set sail from the North Wall in Dublin on what Joyce later termed in *Finnegans Wake* as 'that wildgroup's chase across the kathartic ocean'. He borrowed the fare from Lady Gregory and George Russell, who said that Joyce behaved caddishly and added that a touch of starvation would do him good. In *Ulysses*, Stephen Dedalus remembers he owes money to George Russell (A.E.) when he says 'A.E.I.O.U.' Joyce tried to borrow from Skeffington, who refused, resenting the fact that Joyce had never paid him back previous loans. He thought that Joyce's plan to bring Nora along with him was unfair to her, but before they left he wrote to Joyce sending his best wishes for his welfare. Joyce's

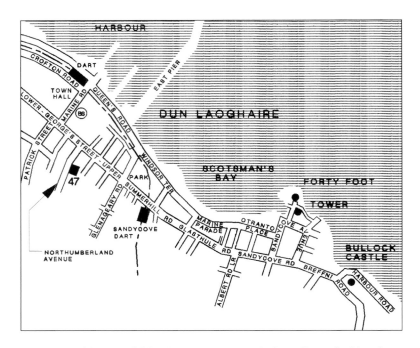

aunt, Josephine, and his sister Margaret tried to dissuade him from taking Nora away with him, but he had already made up his mind.

Aunt Josephine, Margaret, Stanislaus and John Joyce were on the quay to see him off. John Joyce had not been told that Nora was also going. The couple boarded the boat separately, with Joyce going first. He must have had some doubts as to whether Nora might change her mind at the last moment, like the girl in the story 'Eveline', but Nora boarded bravely on her own, with no one to bid her farewell.

They arrived tired and hungry in Zurich to discover that there was no job available; the Berlitz School claimed to be unaware of Joyce's application. The director of the school informed him, however, that there was a vacancy in Pola, which was the principal naval station on the Adriatic. Neither Joyce nor Nora particularly liked Pola; Nora found it a 'queer place'. Joyce managed to earn two pounds a week by teaching English to naval personnel. It was during this time that he had his broadside, a poem of ninety-six lines, entitled 'The Holy Office', printed at his own expense in Pola with Stanislaus responsible for its distribution. Soon Nora was pregnant, and Joyce asked Stanislaus to read some books on mid-wifery and embryology and send him the results. In March 1905 Joyce was transferred to Trieste. For Nora, life became a litany of gloom. She was afraid to go out on her own because the Triestine women were so rude; they used to nudge each other and laugh when they saw her pregnant, in her short cheap skirt with thick hair done over her ears. If she wanted to go out, Joyce had to accompany her and spend whole afternoons looking for simple things at a reasonable price. As soon as her pregnancy became more noticeable, they were turned out of their lodgings. Nora tried unsuccessfully to make baby's clothes from a pattern Joyce's aunt had sent to her.

Their son Giorgio, whose birth they miscalculated by one month, was born on 27 July 1905. Joyce refused to have him baptized. He found the responsibilities of fatherhood difficult to cope with and asked Stanislaus to join them. Nora was relieved at Stanislaus' arrival for not only did he help her financially but he also retrieved Joyce from his drunken bouts in different cafes. Joyce was seized with a desire to escape, recalling the rumour that Ibsen had ended his marriage by leaving his wife. He wrote to his Aunt Josephine to tell her that he was planning to leave Nora, subconsciously knowing that she would dissuade him. Stanislaus helped iron out the crisis between them, and over the next ten years acted as what he later called 'my brother's keeper'. At the end of November 1905 Joyce sent the completed manuscript of *Dubliners* to Grant Richards, a publishers in London. In May 1906 *Chamber Music* was published by Elkin Mathews in London. In July the family and Stanislaus moved to Rome, where Joyce got a job as a foreign correspondent in a bank. He continued drinking and Nora used to threaten that if he didn't give it up she would have the child baptized, but even this had little effect on him. He disliked Rome, and soon they returned to Trieste. Nora was pregnant again and Joyce

Manuscript of poem XXXII from Chamber Music *by Joyce, with autographs of two of his sisters, at 44 Fontenoy Street on 29 August 1909.*

contracted rheumatic fever. He was in the same hospital at the time that his daughter was born in the pauper's wing. The baby, born on St Anne's day, was named Lucia Anna; Lucia being the patron saint of eyesight, and Anna after Nora's mother. On being discharged, Nora was given twenty crowns in charity.

From the time Joyce and Nora had left Dublin in 1904, to his first return visit to Ireland in 1909, they had moved to at least sixteen different addresses, consisting of rooms, flats, hotels and guesthouses.

VI
Return Visits to Dublin, 1909, 1910 and 1912

URING HIS TEN-YEAR sojourn in Trieste, Joyce made three visits to Ireland. The first of these lasted from 29 July to 9 September 1909, when the twenty-five year old Joyce took his small son, Giorgio, with him to meet his grandfather and aunts, who were then living at 44 Fontenoy Street, the smallest house they had so far inhabited. It is an end-of-terrace house, halfway down Fontenoy Street. It has a single storey front, a two-storey back and is a redbrick property comprising two bedrooms, a sitting-room with fireplace, a dining-room, or possibly a third bedroom, and a kitchen with fireplace. It had a small rear garden, approximately twenty-five feet long, which contained a privy. The street in the north city centre is off Mountjoy Street, near Black Church and close to the Royal Canal bank. A spur from the Royal Canal extended three to four miles from the main line, which ran behind Mountjoy Jail in Phibsborough to the Broadstone Railway Station (Midland and Great Western Line), crossing over Phibsborough Road by the Foster Aqueduct. At the time, the area around the station was lively with commerce. There were a number of hotels in the vicinity, none of which now survive. After it became obsolete, Broadstone Harbour was filled in in 1877, the middle section

in 1927, and the final stretch in 1956. This now forms a pleasant green park in the neighbourhood. Nearby is another unusual park which is composed mainly of water, circumvented by a path. This was Blessington Street Reservoir which was opened in 1810 and supplied water to the north side of the city. It also supplied water to Jameson's Distillery in

44 Fontenoy Street, Dublin, where Joyce and his son, Giorgio, stayed in 1909.

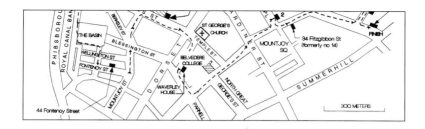

Bow Street until malting stopped there in 1972. The basin is still fed by a two-mile-long pipe that connects to the Royal Canal above the eighth lock. It was originally named the Royal George Reservoir, but has always been referred to by the local people as 'the Basin'. Swans and ducks abound and it contains a good selection of fish, such as rudd, perch, roach and eels. This pleasant little oasis of four acres is nicely landscaped, with interesting plants and is just a stroll from Fontenoy Street.

John Joyce left St Peter's Terrace in May 1905, having sold off what remained of his interest in the house. Margaret, who had run the household for six years, left Fontenoy Street on 20 August 1905 to become a Sister of Mercy in New Zealand, leaving her five sisters May, Eileen, Eva, Florence and Mabel in Fontenoy Street. With six inhabitants, together with Joyce and his son, it did not leave much space in the house. Charles had left the previous year to an unhappy marriage. Joyce felt sorry for the family and made up his mind to do something for them, not that he was in a position to do much. Together with Stanislaus he paid to have Eileen's voice trained. He also planned to take Eva back to Trieste with him but was concerned about how he would pay her fare.

His aunt Josephine thought he had lost his boyishness during his five-year absence from Dublin: George Russell said that he looked like a businessman; his sister Eileen thought he was 'very foreign looking'; others considered him melancholy but everyone agreed that he was very thin. During this visit Joyce met many of his former friends and rivals. Among them were Oliver St John Gogarty, from whom he refused invitations to motor to Enniskerry, and Francis and Hanna Sheehy Skeffington, who pronounced Joyce 'somewhat blasé'. He was interested to learn that the girl for whom he had so much admiration, Mary Sheehy, was to marry his friend Thomas Kettle on 8 September. Joyce did not attend the wedding but arranged to have the couple sent a copy of *Chamber Music.* He invited them to visit Trieste on their honeymoon. He wrote to Nora telling her that he had had a four-hour conversation with his good friend Kettle, saying he was the best friend he had in Ireland. He asked Nora to put the house in order for their visit. Joyce met Cosgrave, who subsequently caused him a lot of pain, alleging that he had been with Nora and telling him that on the evenings in 1904 when she had not been out with Joyce, that he, Cosgrave, had courted her. Joyce was furious; he wrote a couple of disturbed letters to Nora, accusing her of meeting Cosgrave outside the Museum and going with him along the same streets, down by the canal, down to the banks of the River Dodder. Later he was reassured by J.F. Byrne and was satisfied that it was all an untruth. An apology followed to Nora, in which he told her that he was out of his mind with rage at the time and said he was absurdly jealous of her past. He brought Giorgio to visit J.F. Byrne who lived in 7 Eccles Street, which he was to make the home of Leopold Bloom in *Ulysses.*

Joyce visited some editors in Dublin and attended the premiere of Shaw's *The Shewing-Up of Blanco Posnet* at the Abbey Theatre, on the pretext of reviewing it for *Piccolo della Sera* in Trieste. The following day he took the train with Giorgio to visit Mrs Annie Barnacle at 4 Bowling Green in Galway. Nora's uncle, Michael Healy, put Joyce and Giorgio up in his house on Dominick Street. Joyce wanted to see all the places where Nora had lived and spoken about. He visited the house in St Augustine Street where Nora had lived with her grandmother, Catherine Healy, pretending that he wanted to buy it so that he could see the room in which she had slept. In a letter to Nora, written from Bowling Green, he said, 'next year you and I may come here'. This was followed by a letter telling her that he wished her to be surrounded by everything that is fine, 'you are not, as you say, a poor uneducated girl. You are my bride, darling and all I can give you of pleasure and joy in this life I wish to give you.' He got on well with Mrs Barnacle who sang 'The Lass of Aughrim' for him. He had heard Nora sing it and used it in 'The Dead'.

Before returning to Trieste on 9 September, Joyce signed a contract for the publication of *Dubliners* with Maunsel & Co. in Dublin. He took Nora back an expensive piece of jewellery with the inscription from one of his poems 'love is unhappy when love is away'. On his return to Trieste, a chance remark by his sister Eva, prompted Joyce's return again to Dublin in late 1909. She felt homesick and wanted to go back to Dublin but said she would miss the cinema and wasn't it strange that Dublin had none. Joyce found a syndicate of four Triestine businessmen and informed them that he knew of a city of five-hundred-thousand inhabitants, where there was not a single cinema and that if a fast move was made they could capture not only Dublin, but Cork and Belfast too. They were interested in the idea and agreed that Joyce, who had offered to do so, should act as their agent. Joyce returned to Dublin a few weeks later on 21 October to negotiate the setting up of the first cinema in Dublin. Meanwhile Nora was left penniless and threatened with eviction in Trieste, despite the number of love letters to and fro. During this period the frank letters were sent to her. Again, Joyce stayed in Fontenoy Street. Within a week he found premises for the cinema on Mary Street in the city centre. On this visit Joyce did not see many of his friends as he was busy making arrangements for the opening of the Volta Cinema. He worked tirelessly, writing to Stanislaus that they had gone to Cork at 8.00 am and had mooned around for five dreary hours. He was back in Dublin at 11.30 pm and home at midnight and in his rickety bed at 3.00 am Since this work began, he wrote, he had never been to bed before 3.00 or 3.30 am.

He went to the theatre with his father and a sister just a short time before his father was admitted to Jervis Street Hospital with conjunctivitis. Joyce was left to take care of the household at Fontenoy Street. He booked the Triestine businessmen, Messrs Machnich and Rebez, into Finn's Hotel, but wanting to save money they decided to stay instead in rooms above the Volta. Nevertheless, Joyce paid the hotel and whilst doing so asked the waitress to show him Nora's room.

The Cinematograph Volta opened on 20 December, with a report published in the *Evening Telegraph:*

> Yesterday, at 45 Mary Street, a most interesting cinematograph exhibition was opened before a large number of invited visitors. The hall in which the display takes place is most admirably laid out. Indeed, no expense would appear to have been spared in making the entertainment one deserving of the patronage of the public. Perhaps its special feature is that it is of Italian origin, and is in that respect somewhat out of the ordinary and more conventional forms of such displays. For an initial experiment it was remarkably good, remembering how difficult it is to produce, with absolute completeness, a series of pictures at the first stage of their location in new surroundings; the occasion may be described as having been particularly successful. The chief pictures shown were *The First Paris Orphanage*, *La Pourponniere*, and *The Tragic Story of Beatrice Cenci*. The latter, although very ex-cellent, was hardly as exhilarating a subject as one would desire on the eve of the festive season. But it was very much appreciated and applauded. An excellent little string orchestra played charmingly during the afternoon. Mr James Joyce, who is in charge of the exhibition, has worked apparently indefatigably in its production and deserves to be congratulated on the success of the inaugural exhibition.

The Volta Cinema in Mary Street, which Joyce was instrumental in setting up.

During this visit, Joyce was appointed the Triestine agent for Irish tweed by the Dublin Woollen Company and he sent twelve yards of Donegal tweed to Nora. He also boasted that he had clothed some of his pupils in Irish homespuns.

In a letter to Stanislaus on 23 December, Joyce wrote that he was taking Eileen back to Trieste with him: 'This is such a dreadful house that it is a God's act to rescue Eileen from it. Let us try to manage it.' The letter ends, 'Help your poor sister!' Wishing to return to Trieste and unwilling to act as Manager of the Volta, Joyce bought Eileen a warm coat and gloves and they left for Trieste on 2 January 1910. He had no further connection with the Volta and left the running of it to Messrs Machnich, Rebez and Novak. Soon after, the Volta was sold to the British Provincial Cinematograph Theatres Ltd. Within a year they had cinemas in Sackville Street and Grafton Street.

In July 1910 Maunsel & Co. postponed the publication of *Dubliners*. On 15 July 1912 Joyce returned to Dublin for his final visit and remained for almost three months, departing on 11 September. The purpose of his visit concerned the proposed publication of *Dubliners*. Nora and Lucia travelled ahead, arriving in Dublin on 8 July, where they were met at Westland Row Station by John Joyce, Charles, Eva and Florence. John Joyce brought them all to Finn's Hotel, where Nora was delighted to return as a guest. She then travelled to Galway to stay with her family whom she had not seen for eight years.

Joyce and Giorgio followed a week later. When passing through London, they called to the London office of Maunsel & Co. and also visited W.B. Yeats who gave them tea and fruit. Joyce spent two days having discussions with his publishers in Dublin before going to Galway. Here he stayed at 4 Bowling Green with Nora and the children. They also visited Nora's uncle, Michael Healy, who lived in Dominick Street. He looked after them well and fed them 'in great style'. In a letter to Stanislaus, Joyce wrote that he had come so far he had better stay a little longer if possible. Nora and Joyce went to the races and visited the Aran Islands off the Galway coast, where Joyce wrote two articles for the Italian newspaper *Piccolo della Sera*. He spent a lot of time out in the air, rowing. He cycled to Oughterard and visited the cemetery, where he discovered a headstone bearing the inscription 'J. Joyce'.

When he was at Galway, Stanislaus wrote from Trieste informing him that the landlord wanted his rent. But Stanislaus was left to find another flat at 4 Via Donato Bramante and to move all the Joyce belongings to it.

21 Richmond Place.

A letter from George Roberts, the managing director of Maunsel &
Co. brought Joyce hurrying back to Dublin. He left Nora and the children
behind to save on expenses and from 17 to 22 August stayed at 17
Richmond Place. Roberts wanted changes made to some of the stories
in *Dubliners.* Joyce approached two of his friends for assistance. Kettle

proved unresponsive but C.P. Curran willingly agreed to speak to Roberts on behalf of Joyce. In the meantime Joyce wrote to Nora, in a letter postmarked 22 August, informing her that he had taken a nice double-bedded room at the front of the house at 21 Richmond Place on the North Circular Road. He rented this from 22 August until 11 September. He was hoping to go around with her during Horse Show Week and wanted to show her the many places in Dublin that were mentioned in his book. He said he was foolish enough to hope that they might be able to spend some happy days together after all the trouble with the publisher.

Having made some concessions with the stories, Joyce refused to make any further changes and on 23 August he received a letter from Roberts saying that Maunsel & Co. had been advised that actions for libel would be brought if public houses, railway companies or any going concerns were mentioned by name in the text. The outcome of the meetings and correspondence proved totally unsatisfactory for Joyce. He wrote to Nora again saying that he walked down the streets feeling the whole future of his life was slipping out of his grasp. Nora and the children joined him in Dublin where they stayed with the Murrays on the North Strand, Joyce having left his rented room at 21 Richmond Place four days before. In the end, the sheets of *Dubliners* were destroyed by Roberts because of the 'objectionable' passages in some of the stories. Joyce, having no further business in the city, left Dublin for Trieste with his family on 11 September 1912. This was to be Joyce's last visit to Ireland. The family crossed to Flushing in Holland, and, while in a station waiting-room, Joyce wrote a second broadside entitled 'Gas from a Burner'. He had it printed in Trieste and sent it back to his brother, Charles, for distribution in Dublin.

His pattern of address changing did not stop when he left Ireland and continued until his death. He did not forget his Dublin addresses, most of which are transmuted by his Homeric humour in *Finnegans Wake*:

Letter, carried of Shaun, son of Hek, written of Shem, brother of Shaun, uttered for Alp, mother of Shem, for Hek, father of Shaun. Initialled. Gee. Gone. 29 Hardware Saint. Lendet till Laonum. Baile-Atha-Cliath. 31 Jan. 1132 A.D. Here Commerces Enville. Tried Apposite House. 13 Fitzgibbets. Loco. Dangerous. Tax 9d. B.L. Guineys, esqueer. L.B. Not known at 1132 a. 12 Norse Richmound. Nave unlodgeable. Loved noa's dress. Sinned, Jetty Pierrse. Noon sick parson. 92 Windsewer. Ave. No such no. Vale. Finn's Hot. Exbelled from 1014 d. Pulldown. Fearview. Opened by Miss Take. 965 nighumpledan sextiffits. Shout at site. Roofloss. Fit Dunlop and Be Satisfied. Mr Domnall O'Domnally. Q.V. 8 Royal Terrors. None so strait. Shutter up. Dining with the Danes. Removed to Philip's Burke. At sea. D.E.D. Place scent on. Clontalk. Father Jacob, Rice Factor. 3 Castlewoos. P.V. Arrusted. J.P. Converted to Hospitalism. Ere the March past of Civilisation. Once Bank of Ireland's. Return to City Arms. 2 Milchbroke. Wrongly spilled. Traumcondraws. Now Bunk of England's. Drowned in the Laffey. Here. The Reverest Adam Foundlitter. Shown geshotten. 7 Streetpetres. Since Cabranke. Seized of the Crownd. Well, Sir Arthur. Buy Patersen's Matches. Unto his promisk hands. Blown up last Lemmas by Orchid Lodge. Search Unclaimed Male. House Condamned by Ediles. Back in Few Minutes. Closet for Repeers. 60 Shellburn. Key at Kate's. Kiss. Issac's Butt, Poor Man. Dalicious arson. Caught. Missing. Justiciated. Kainly forewarred. Abraham Badly's King, Park Bogey. Salved. All reddy berried. Hollow and eavy. Desert it. Overwayed.

Understrumped. Back to the P.O. Kaer of. Ownes owe M.O. Too Let. To Be Soiled. Cohabited by Unfortunates. Lost all Licence. His Bouf Toe is Frozen Over. X,Y and Z, Ltd, Destinied Tears. A.B, ab, Sender. Boston (Mass). 31 Jun. 13, 12.P.D. Razed. Lawyered. Vacant. Mined. Here's the Bayleaffs. Step out to Hall out of that, Ereweaker, with your Bloody Big Bristol. Bung. Stop. Bung. Stop. Cumm Bumm. Stop. Came Baked to Auld Aireen. Stop.

VII
Epilogue:
The Continental Experience

AFTER HIS FINAL VISIT to Dublin in 1912, Joyce and his family returned to Trieste where they remained with Stanislaus and Eileen for the next three years in the apartment in which Stanislaus had found in the Via Donato Bramante. Joyce continued to teach English at a commercial school and to give private tuiton.

By 1913 Joyce had started work on his play, *Exiles*, and the same year, following correspondence with Yeats, he contacted Dora Marsden through American poet Ezra Pound. She was editor of the *Egoist*, and agreed to publish *A Portrait* in serial form in her review. In March 1914 Joyce began to write *Ulysses* and in June *Dubliners* was finally published by Grant Richards in London.

In April 1915 Eileen married Frantisek Schaurek, a Czech bank cashier, and the couple went to live in Prague. With the outbreak of the First World War, Stanislaus, as an enemy alien, was interned and Joyce thought it wise to move with his family to neutral Switzerland. Arriving penniless in Zurich, Joyce, now aged thirty-three, was pleased to receive some money from Nora's uncle, Michael Healy, which tided them over for a period. They spent most of the war years in Zurich, remaining there for some time after the armistice. Joyce wrote much of

Ulysses in Switzerland. While he was there his financial position improved dramatically. He also began to gain a reputation as an author. In 1915 he received a grant from the Royal Literary Fund, a small subsidy from the Society of Authors and a Civil List Grant. Together with these and some royalties, two benefactors appeared on the scene: an English woman, Harriet Shaw Weaver, who worked with Miss Marsden and Edith Rockefeller McCormack, a wealthy American, then living in Zurich.

In 1916 *A Portrait of an Artist as a Young Man* was published by B.W. Huebsch in New York. The following year Joyce had his first eye operation, which was to be followed by eleven more during the next fifteen years. Two years later, Joyce met Frank Budgen, the sanguine and humorous English painter and writer, who was to become an intimate friend of the family. He told Budgen that in *Ulysses* he wanted to give a picture of Dublin so complete that if the city disappeared it could be reconstructed from his book. When Budgen told Joyce that he was writing a book on the composition of *Ulysses*, Joyce was sceptical. He changed his mind when he read the proofs and congratulated Budgen: 'I never knew you could write so well: it must be due to your association with me.' During his last two years in Zurich, *Exiles* was published in London and part of *Ulysses* was serialised both in the *Little Review* in New York and in the *Egoist* in London. During their five years sojourn in Zurich, the Joyce family moved nine times.

In 1919 the family moved back to Trieste but did not remain there very long. Joyce found that the place had changed; Stanislaus noted that Joyce was just as intemperate as ever, and was no longer prepared to act as his guardian.

It was under Ezra Pound's influence that the Joyces moved to Paris in July 1920. Here, there was an audience awaiting him; an admirer lent him his apartment free of rent for a few months and within three days of his arrival he met Sylvia Beach who owned the bookshop, Shakespeare & Co. Although she had never published a book before, she offered to publish *Ulysses* under her own imprint and Joyce agreed. He had bits and pieces to finish off and wrote to his aunt Josephine Murray with various questions. He wanted information on whether or not there any trees behind the Star of the Sea Church in Sandymount, and if there were steps leading down at the side of it from Leahy's Terrace; he also enquired if she remembered the cold February of 1893, and if the canal had frozen over and if people had been skating on it. He had a query concerning J.F. Byrne's former home; he had observed the athletic Byrne climbing over the railings at 7 Eccles Street, and he wished to know if it were possible for an ordinary person to climb over the railings of the house, either from the path or the steps, lowering himself down from the lowest part of the railings till his feet were two or three feet off the ground, and drop unhurt into the area. He needed the information checked in order to finish off a paragraph. He also asked his aunt to write in a notebook all she remembered of the 'curious types' he had known as a child. In Paris, a coterie of friends such as Adrienne Monnier and Valery Larbaud surrounded him and helped to publicize *Ulysses*, published on Joyce's fortieth birthday, 2 February 1922.

The Joyces' home life remained unsettled by their constant moving. Like his father, Joyce found it hard to settle in any particular place for very long; he drifted from one apartment to another, much to the annoyance of Nora. This haphazard and nomadic way of living was causing tension between him and Nora. Against Joyce's wishes, Nora brought her children on a visit to Galway in 1922. The civil war was in progress and fighting flared up in the city. Nora returned to Paris immediately. She never again considered leaving Joyce. Joyce continued to drink and on occasion would have to be escorted home in a taxi by a friend. He realized that he had inherited this trait from his father, and in his later years took steps to control it. He would not drink before evening, and sometimes drank only lime-blossom or vervain tea.

In the spring of 1923 Joyce stated writing *Finnegans Wake*, but this was hampered to some extent by his continuing eye problems, and also by the attitude of some of his friends towards this work. Stanislaus referred to it as a 'drivelling rigmarole'. As a result, there was a falling off of some friendships but these were soon replaced by others who were more open to literary innovations. New friendships were formed with people like Samuel Beckett, Eugene and Maria Jolas, Louis Gillet, Paul and Lucy Leon, Stuart Gilbert and Nino Frank.

With the death of his aunt Josephine, in 1924, a link with Dublin was severed. She was, perhaps, the person closest to Joyce in his youth, especially after his mother's death. To keep on update on Dublin, Joyce now sent his friends to interview his father and to question him about family history and changes in the city. John Joyce was not nearly as efficient as Aunt Josephine had been, but he did his best to cooperate. Occasionally, he found some of the questions put to him rather inane, and asked an interviewer, 'Is Jim mad entirely?' in the course of a conversation he had with Arthur Power in Paris, Joyce remarked: '… I know when I was writing *Ulysses* I tried to give the colour and tone of Dublin with my words; the drab, yet glistening atmosphere of Dublin, its hallucinatory vapours, its tattered confusion, the atmosphere of its bars, its social immobility; they could only be conveyed by the texture of my words. Thought and plot are not so important as some would make them out to be.'

On 4 July 1931, for what he claimed to be merely testamentary reasons, Joyce married Nora in London. His son, Giorgio, married Helen Kastor Fleischman on 10 December, and his father, John Joyce, died on 9 December in the same year. The following February his grandson, Stephen, was born. This prompted Joyce to write his moving poem 'Ecce Puer'. There was a serious problem developing with Lucia's health. In the early thirties, she was showing signs of schizophrenia, which Joyce blamed on himself. For seven years he endeavoured to find a cure for her, bringing her to various doctors. She spent long spells in sanatoriums.

Visitors to Joyce in Paris, in his later years, have spoken of his great interest in hearing news from Dublin. He spoke of it constantly; he told a friend in 1937, 'I never really left it. I carry it around with me.' Constantine Curran, who met Joyce when they were both students at University College and who remained a close friend until Joyce's death, recalled visiting him in Paris and seeing pictures on the walls of Anna Liffey and paintings by Jack B. Yeats. Above all, he remembered a great wood-carving of the Arms of Dublin. Joyce would sing old Tudor songs and Dublin street ballads in an admirable tenor voice. During the visit, Joyce inquired about Dublin and his acquaintances; he loved to reconstruct the different streets, in the precise order of houses, shops and their occupants. When Curran asked him when he was coming back to Dublin, Joyce replied, 'Why should I, have I ever left it?' And, as Curran commented, Joyce never really had. He contained Dublin. His knowledge of the town by inheritance, by observation, by memory, was prodigious, and he was at pains to keep his picture of it up to date. In one of his Paris apartments, Joyce kept a number of Phoenix palms to which he attached a great importance; he said that the plants reminded him of the Phoenix Park.

With the outbreak of the Second World War in 1939 Joyce removed Lucia from Paris, for her safety, to a Maison Sante near La Baule. The Joyces then returned to Paris to find that Giorgio's wife had had a breakdown, so they took their grandson to Mrs Jolas' Ecole Bilingue, in a village called Saint-Gérand-Le-Puy. In December 1939 they left Paris after nineteen years, and moved to the village to be near Stephen. In May *Finnegans Wake* had been published in New York and London.

War again constrained the Joyce family to return to Zurich on 13 December 1940, when they fled from France. Lucia remained behind and Joyce planned to arrange her transfer later to Switzerland. This was to be their final move. They were met at the station by their good friend Carola Giedion-Welcker, the art critic. She was very moved by their appearance; they looked 'like some of the angular figures in a

Picasso drawing, huddled together on the platform. Their clothes had grown too large for them and hung loosely about their forms. They looked pale and undernourished, yet Joyce was in good form.' On arrival, one of the first things he did was to write to the Mayor of Zurich in his most elaborate German, thanking him for the refuge the city had offered to his family and himself. Joyce visited all his old haunts, bringing his little grandson Stephen with him. Every street was familiar to him and the place was cheerful with all the shops lighted and decorated for Christmas. He was happy to be back, walking on the Bahnhofstrasse, the street which inspired his poem of that name and which is included in *Pomes Penyeach*, dated Zurich, 1918.

The family spent a comfortable Christmas with the Giedion-Welckers, where Joyce sang and danced his famous spider-dance. He performed his customary party piece which was kicking his black felt hat into the air until he had finally knocked the bottom out of it. Joyce went to one of his favourite Zurich restaurants, the Kronenhalle, on 7 January 1941. Possibly it was a premonition which prompted his remark, 'Perhaps I won't be here much longer' to the kind proprietess, Frau Zumsteg. Two days later he returned there to celebrate the birthday of a friend, Paul Ruggiero. That night he was overcome with severe abdominal pains. On 10 January he entered a Zurich hospital, the Schwesterhaus Vom Roten Kreuz, not knowing how he could pay the expenses. A duodenal ulcer was diagnosed and an operation was performed that same morning. It was too late and on 13 January Joyce died aged fifty-eight years old. Carola Giedion-Welcker, with Nora's permission, arranged for the casting of a death mask, which was taken by the sculptor Paul Speck. On the tightly closed lips there is the faint trace of a smile.

As in Joyce's short story 'The Dead', his journey westward was accomplished. On 15 January his remains were borne to the wooded and beautiful Fluntern Cemetery high up on the Zurichberg. The snow fell as Nora, her son Giorgio and the Zurich intellectual élite said a final goodbye to Joyce. Tributes were paid both in English and in German over the bier in Friedhofkappelle. Lord Derwent, the British Minister to Berne spoke first and gave a fiting and moving eulogy. He said he had come to bury a great European figure and considered it 'eminently suitable that this cosmopolitan gathering should be assembled here today to bid a last farewell to a man who wherever domiciled … seems to have no creative thought in his mind that was not intimately connected with the Ireland of his birth.' Lord Derwent recalled that he had been in Paris when *Ulysses* first appeared and that he would never forget the stimulating shock of a first acquaintance with it. He remembered Joyce's dreamy, shadowy figure, as if emerging from the Celtic twilight and saw him many times coming out of Sylvia Beach's bookshop in the Rue l'Odeon. He recalled how in later years he had seen Joyce sweep into Fouquet's on the Champs Elysees, 'his eyes vague behind those tragic spectacles, his wilful chin stuck well forward, while the whisper went round carrying his name'.

Ireland was not represented at the funeral.

Nora continued to live in Zurich in relative poverty. To make ends meet, she had to sell most of Joyce's manuscripts and also her jewellery. She developed arthritis, and led a quiet life, visiting the cemetery once a week and receiving the occasional visitor. When asked why she chose to remain in Zurich, she replied that it was because Joyce was there and added, 'I'd like to have a cottage in Ireland, but the Irish don't like Joyce, so there you are.'

Nora died ten years after Joyce and was buried some distance from her husband. As Richard Ellmann remarked, ' the casualness of their lodgings in life was kept after death'. However, in December 1965 they were reinterred together in a grave donated by the city of Zurich. On Bloomsday 1966 the city council of Zurich held a ceremony to mark the unveiling of a bronze memorial over Joyce's grave by the American sculptor Milton Hebald.

Joyce had found his final resting-place.

VIII
How to Get There

ALL THE JOYCE HOUSES are in Dublin City, or within easy reach of the city by either bus or the DART (Dublin Area Rapid Transit). Some of the more common buses serving the routes are indicated. For further information consult the current bus timetable. For the sake of convenience, three tours have been set out that incorporate all of the Joyce houses, along with a tour of Nora's Galway. The tours involve some walking, so wear comfortable shoes.

MALAHIDE
PORTMARNOCK
HOWTH JUNCTION
KILBARRACK
RAHENY
HARMONSTOWN
KILLESTER
CLONTARF ROAD
CONNOLLY STATION
TARA STREET
PEARSE STATION
GRAND CANAL DOCK
LANSDOWNE ROAD
SANDYMOUNT
SYDNEY PARADE
BOOTERSTOWN
BLACKROCK
MONKSTOWN / SEAPOINT
SALTHILL
DUN LAOGHAIRE
SANDYCOVE / GLASTHULE
GLENAGEARY
DALKEY
KILLINEY
SHANKILL
BRAY
GREYSTONES

BAYSIDE
SUTTON
HOWTH

DART
DUBLIN AREA RAPID TRANSIT

Route 1   *(See maps on pages 13, 55, 58)*

Time taken:	3 hours approximately

Destination:	23 Castlewood Avenue, Rathmines (10-minute ride).
Bus number:	15 or 15A
Depart:	College Street.
Alight:	At Swan Centre, which is the stop beyond Rathmines Town Hall. Continue to walk in the same direction the bus has gone; take the first turning into Castlewood Avenue. Number 23 is situated on the third corner on the right, at the intersection of Castlewood Avenue and Cambridge Road.

Destination:	Church of the Three Patrons, Rathgar (8-minute ride).
Bus number:	15 or 15A. Retrace your steps to the bus stop at which you alighted.
Alight:	Three stops ahead of the Swan Centre, at the church. Have a walk around this typical nineteenth-century church, where John Stanislaus Joyce and Mary Jane Murray sang in the choir together. Notice the side altars and fine organ loft.

Destination:	41 Brighton Square, Rathgar, birthplace of James Joyce. Continue to walk in the same direction the bus has gone. Proceed along Rathgar Road; take the first turn right, up Garville Avenue. Continue straight across Rathgar Avenue, along Garville Avenue Upper. Reaching Brighton Square, continue straight along the side of it passing the Victorian pillar-box. Turn right; number 41 is the eighth house down on the left-hand side.

Destination:	Site of 2 Millbourne Avenue, Drumcondra (38-minute ride).
Bus number:	16 or 16A
Depart:	Harold's Cross Road. From number 41 Brighton Square, retrace your steps back as far as the corner of the square. Turn right. Traverse Harold's Cross Road to the bus stop a few paces down. Take the bus and after a few minutes it will cross the Grand Canal. Shortly afterwards, on your right-hand side, you can see number 52 Clanbrassil Street, the home of Leopold Bloom. It is marked by a plaque. This bus goes through the city centre. (If leaving from city centre for Drumcondra, take the 16 or 16A going northbound from Upper O'Connell Street.)
Alight:	The first stop after Drumcondra Bridge, Drumcondra Road Upper. Walk back a few paces in the direction of the bridge; take the first turn right up Millbourne Avenue, and walk up alongside the grey stone wall. Number 2 Millbourne Avenue has been replaced by the apartment block on the right-hand side.
Destination:	10 Glengariff Parade (formerly number 32 Glengariff Parade).
Bus number:	16 or 16A. Retrace steps back and cross Drumcondra Bridge. Cross to the far side of Drumcondra Road Lower, and take the bus three stops down.
Alight:	Dorset Street at North Circular Road corner. Cross Dorset Street and walk back a few paces; turn left up Innisfallen Parade and reaching the top of it turn left. Number 10 Glengariff Parade is on the far side of the street down towards the North Circular Road.

Destination:	7 St Peter's Terrace, now 5 St Peter's Road. Continue to the end of Glengariff Parade; turn right into the North Circular Road. Using the spire of St Peter's Church as your guide, you will pass, on your right, the John Doyle Pub. Cross straight over, through the lights at Phibsborough Road; take the right-hand fork at the church; then take the first turn right into St Peter's Road. Number 7 St Peter's Terrace was renumbered 5 St Peter's Road and is the third house on the left-hand side.
Destination:	44 Fontenoy Street. Retrace your steps crossing back across Phibsborough Road through the traffic lights. About 100 yards farther on the right-hand side there is an unobtrusive grey military memorial on a plinth consisting of a soldier, which is dedicated to the Irish Volunteers. This is situated at the top of a narrow linear park, named Royal Canal Bank. (It was once a spur connecting the Royal Canal with Broadstone Railway Station.) Descend the steps and turn sharp left into the park. Continue on through this park until reaching a grassy circular mound in the pathway. Proceed left through the gate in the wall which is an entrance to Blessington Basin. Bear right around the basin until reaching a similar type gate. Exit through this; continue straight, and take the second turn left to Fontenoy Street. Number 44 is 50 yards down on the left-hand side.
Destination:	7 Eccles Street. Retrace steps to the basin and continue around, exiting

at its main gate to Blessington Street; proceed left, then right, up Nelson Street, or, continue straight down Fontenoy Street to Mountjoy Street; turn left and proceed up the junction of Blessington and Berkeley Street. Cross the junction and turn right up Nelson Street; turn right into Eccles Street. On the left is the Mater Misericordiae Hospital and on the right, St George's Church. Number 7 Eccles Street was roughly where the main entrance of the new private clinic to the Mater Hospital is situated.

Destination: Hardwicke Street.
Continue down Eccles Street, crossing straight over Dorset Street into Hardwicke Place. Turn right into Hardwicke Street. Number 29 has been demolished; note number 4 Waverley House, on the left-hand side, which was featured in Joyce's story 'The Boarding House'.

Destination: Fitzgibbon Street.
Turn left into North Frederick Street and left again into Gardiner Row and straight into Great Denmark Street where Belvedere College is situated on the left-hand side. (Opposite the main entrance to Belvedere College is North Great George's Street, where, at number 35, the James Joyce Centre is situated.)
Proceed straight into Gardiner Place; cross over to Mountjoy Square North and to Belvedere Place, here number 2 was the home of the Sheehys. Proceed up Fitzgibbon Street, where the Joyce home, number 14 and now renumbered as 34, may be seen on the right-hand side of the street.

Destination:	13 North Richmond Street.
	Continue down to the traffic lights on the North Circular Road; bear right; take the third turn on the left to North Richmond Street. Number 13 is on the right-hand side. Retrace steps back to North Circular Road; turn left for numbers 17 and 21 Richmond Place which now forms part of the North Circular Road. Numbers 17 and 21 are now numbers 609 and 617 respectively.

Route 2 *(See maps on pages 41, 99, 128)*

Time taken:	3 hours approximately
Destination:	60 Shelbourne Road, Ballsbridge (10-minute ride).
Bus number:	7 or 7A
Depart:	O'Connell Street (going southbound).
Alight:	On Northumberland Road at the stop after Haddington Road. Walk back; turn right down Haddington Road, passing Beggar's Bush Barracks (now housing the National Print Museum and the Geological Survey of Ireland), to the traffic lights at the junction of Shelbourne Road; turn right. Number 60 is about 200 metres up on the left-hand side at the bend of the road. There is a plaque on the house, which mentions the Joyce connection.
Destination:	22 Dromard Terrace, Sandymount (1-mile walk. 20 minutes).
	Continue walking along Shelbourne Road. At traffic lights turn left down Lansdowne Road. Continue

down to the end of Herbert Road and at T-junction take a right turn into Tritonville Road. Take first left turn into Claremont Road and proceed to the end. Cross straight over Sandymount Road to Seafort Avenue. On reaching the island in Seafort Avenue bear left and 22 Dromard Terrace is a few paces down on the right-hand side. There is a plaque on the house, which reads:

James Joyce
Stayed here on 16th June 1904
The day on which
He set his novel
Ulysses

Destination: Blackrock Park and 23 Carysfort Avenue, Blackrock. Retrace steps to Gilford Road; then turn right up Sandymount Avenue to the DART Station (15-minute walk approximately). Take the southbound train.

Alight: Blackrock Station. To visit Blackrock Park, turn right coming out of the station exit, and proceed down the lane that runs parallel to the railway track, to a side entrance. For Carysfort Avenue, turn left out of the station exit, then turn right up Bath Place to the main street in Blackrock; turn left and pass the old, stone, market cross of Blackrock, then turn up Carysfort Avenue, crossing the intersecting Frescati Road, to the continuation of Carysfort Avenue. Number 23 is the first house on the left-hand side.

Destination: 47 Northumberland Avenue, Dun Laoghaire. If you prefer less walking, take a 10-minute bus ride on the number 7 or 7A from the stop in Blackrock Main Street situated at the top of Bath Place. Alight at Marine Road, Dun Laoghaire; otherwise, take the DART from Blackrock Station three stops on to Dun Laoghaire. Cross road and proceed up to the top of Marine Road; turn left into George's Street Upper; take second turn right to Northumberland Avenue. Number 47 is on the left-hand side opposite the Methodist Church.

Destination:	James Joyce Tower, Sandycove. (30-minute walk from Northumberland Avenue to the Joyce Tower). Retrace steps to George's Street Upper. Cross the street and walk back to seafront. Continue southwards along the coast road to Newtownsmith, turning left down Sandycove Avenue West, which leads to Sandycove. Take the path seaward alongside it, passing a white house, circular in shape, which blends in with the architecture of the Martello Tower, which is directly behind it. You will pass the famous Forty-Foot Bathing Place on the left-hand side as you proceed towards the Tower.
Opening hours:	The Tower is open daily from March to October (Monday–Saturday, 10 am–1 pm, 2 pm–5 pm; Sunday 2 pm–6 pm) and by appointment during the rest of the year. Tel: (01) 2809265. email: joycetower@dublintourism.ie
Destination:	1 Martello Terrace, Bray.
Depart:	Take the southbound DART from Sandycove Station.
Alight:	Five stops ahead at Bray. Cross the level-crossing towards the Esplanade. Turn left. You will see Martello

Terrace at the end, facing you. It is a 6-minute walk
from the station to number 1 Martello Terrace, which
is at the 'sea' end. See also Vance & Wilson, Chemist,
founded in 1860, 92 Main Street, Bray. Return to the
station to take the DART back to the city. The journey
is approximately 30 minutes.

Route 3   *(See map on page 72)*

Time taken:	Less than 1 hour

Destination:	29 Windsor Avenue, Fairview (10-minute ride).
Bus Numbers:	31 or 130
Depart:	Lower Abbey Street, City Centre.
Alight:	At Annesley Bridge. Make a U-turn into Fairview Strand. Take first turn right up Windsor Avenue. Number 29 is about 250 yards on the left-hand side.

Destination:	8 Royal Terrace, now Inverness Road.
	Retrace steps. On reaching Fairview Strand turn right. Take the next turn right, up Philipsburgh Avenue and the second left up Melrose Avenue. Inverness Road forms a T-junction with Melrose Avenue. Number 8 is slightly to the right, facing you. Cross the road, and turn left, then right, around the back lane behind the houses. This lane is substantially as it was in Joyce's time. Follow the course of the lane and you will come out at the far end of Inverness Road.

Destination:	Richmond Avenue.
	Retrace your steps back by Melrose Avenue and

Philipsburgh Avenue and turn right along Fairview Strand. Proceed up to the traffic lights and bear right up Richmond Road. The first turn right is Richmond Avenue where the Joyces lived, but the house has been demolished.

Destination:	Convent Avenue.

This is the next turn right. It is not known for certain which house the Joyce family occupied, but it was probably the house on the corner. The entrance to St Vincent's Hospital, which backs on to Inverness Road, is at the end of Convent Avenue. Retrace your steps via Fairview Strand back to Annesley Bridge and cross the road to get a bus back to the city. (If you wish to visit Dollymount Strand on North Bull Island, take a number 30 bus at the stop from which you alighted in Fairview. It is a short bus ride; alight at the Bull Wall.)

Route 4 *(See map on page 105)*

Time taken:	1½ to 2 hours approximately
Destination:	Nora Barnacle's Galway.
Depart:	The easiest way to get to Galway by public transport is by train from Heuston Station in Dublin. For information concerning train times consult the Iarnród Éireann website at www.irishrail.ie. Consult the timetable for Dublin/Galway/ Westport.
Alight:	Ceannt Station in Galway, turn left out of the station

exit and proceed straight down alongside Eyre
Square; turn right to see number 2 Prospect Hill,
where Nora and her friend, Mary O'Holleran, bought
sweets in Mr Bodkin's shop. This is now an Off-
Licence, beside Richardson's Public House. Nora's
parents also lived in the Prospect Hill area sometime
between 1882 and 1886.

Retrace your steps to the corner of Prospect Hill,
and continue in a straight line alongside Eyre Square
to Williamsgate Street; turn right down Eglinton
Street. The firm of Joe Young, who manufactured
mineral water, was sited here where Wille Mulvagh,
Nora's boyfriend, worked. (If you wish to see Shop
Street, go down William Street and you will reach
Shop Street. Number 33 was formerly the site of
O'Gorman's bookshop where Nora's sister, Kathleen,
worked. Joyce sent the owner a signed copy of *Ulysses*.)

Continue straight to Francis Street and note the
Franciscan Abbey Church, known as 'the Abbey' on
the left side. This is where Nora attended devotions,
and where in 1935, her uncle, Michael Healy died
while attending Mass. The Convent of Mercy Primary
School is on the right at the top of Francis Street as
you come up past the Abbey Church. This school is
on the same site as the old one Nora attended. The
original was demolished over twenty years ago.

Turn left into St Vincent's Avenue, and left again
into Newtownsmyth. At the end of Newtownsmyth
pause and have a look down Mary Street where
Thomas Barnacle had rooms. This was to be his last
home. Willie Mullvagh lived in number 2, which is
now demolished.

Take a right turn into Bowling Green and view number 8, the Nora Barnacle House. It is now a museum devoted to James and Nora Joyce and is run by two Galway sisters, Sheila and Mary Gallagher. It is open from May to September or by appointment. (For further information telephone 091 564 743.)

Continue left up Market Street, then right to Upper Abbeygate Street. At the corner of Lower Abbeygate Street and Middle Street is a shopping complex in what was formerly St Nicholas' Pro-Cathedral, where Nora made her First Communion. The first left turn brings you onto Whitehall, where Catherine Healy, Nora's maternal grandmother, lived with her son, Thomas, later to be Nora's guardian. Annie and Thomas Barnacle, Nora's parents, also lived with them for a while after they were married.

Continue down St Augustine Street, where Catherine Healy later lived. Turn right up Cross Street, then left across O'Brien's Bridge; turn right to Nun's Island, which appears in 'The Dead' as the home of Gretta's grandmother. There is no evidence that Catherine Healy ever lived here, though Nora's paternal grandmother may have done. It is an interesting area and formerly the site of a number of mills. Retrace your steps back from Nun's Island Street and turn right. Proceed to the top of Mill Street to the Presentation Convent where Nora worked as a portress. Continue, taking the first turning right, along Canal Road Upper to University Road. Turn left, then right into the main entrance of University College where Sonny Bodkin was a student. View the original building.

Retrace your steps, turning left at the end of the avenue. Continue along University Road over Beggar's Bridge, passing St Nicholas' Cathedral on your right. Cross Salmon Weir Bridge; turn left up around Waterside, then take a right turn down Corrib Terrace and Wood Quay. It was from this point that Joyce went boating on the River Corrib during his visit in 1912. Return to Eyre Square via Eglinton Street and Williamsgate Street.

Destination:	Rahoon Cemetery (10–15 minute ride).
Bus Number:	33 or 34
Depart:	The main bus stop is in the city centre at Debenhams, just off Eyre Square.
Alight:	Outside Rahoon Cemetery. Enter cemetery through the old gate and follow the path straight ahead; Michael Bodkin's grave, which is a vault-like structure rising four feet above the ground, is the third on the left-hand side. Close by, Nora's father lies buried in Section G, Row 14, No.5. A simple headstone of limestone marks his grave. On it is inscribed:

Thomas Barnacle
Died 13th July 1921
Aged 75 years.
Rest in Peace

Chronology of James Joyce's Dublin Addresses

5 May 1880
John Stanislaus Joyce married Mary Jane Murray

1880–1
13 Ontario Terrace, Rathmines, 30 Emorville Road off the South Circular Road and 47 Northumberland Avenue, Dun Laoghaire, the first homes of Mr and Mrs John Stanislaus Joyce

1882–4
41 Brighton Square, Rathgar. Birthplace of James Joyce

1884–7
23 Castlewood Avenue, Rathmines

May 1887–91
1 Martello Terrace, Bray, County Wicklow

September 1888 – December 1892
Clongowes Wood College, Sallins, County Kildare

Early 1892–3
'Leoville', 23 Carysfort Avenue, Blackrock

Early 1893–4
29 Hardwicke Street
14 Fitzgibbon Street (renumbered 34)

1893–8
Belvedere College

1894
2 Millbourne Avenue, Drumcondra

Late 1894/early 1895–7
13 North Richmond Street

1897 – May 1899
29 Windsor Avenue, Fairview

1898–1902
University College

1899
Convent Avenue, Fairview

1899 – April 1900
13 Richmond Avenue, Fairview

May 1900–01
8 Royal Terrace, Fairview

Summer 1900
Trip to Mullingar

1901–02
32 Glengariff Parade, Dublin

24 October 1902 – 17 January 1903
7 St Peter's Terrace, Phibsborough [Cabra]

23 January – 11 April 1903
Paris

12 April 1903 – late March 1904
7 St Peter's Terrace, Phibsborough

Late March – 31 August 1904
60 Shelbourne Road, Ballsbridge

16 June & 1–2 September 1904
22 Dromard Terrace, Sandymount (with James H. Cousins)

4–8 September
The Martello Tower, Sandycove (with Oliver St John Gogarty)

8 October 1904
Departed from Ireland with Nora Barnacle

Return Visits

29 July – 26 August 1909
44 Fontenoy Street

26–27 August 1909
Day trip to Galway (4 Bowling Green)

28 August – 9 September 1909 & 21 October 1909 – 2 January 1910
44 Fontenoy Street

17 July – 17 August 1912
Galway

17–22 August 1912
17 Richmond Place, North Circular Road (now 609 North Circular Road)

22 August – 11 September 1912
21 Richmond Place, North Circular Road (now 617 North Circular Road)

Useful Information

Dublin Bus/Bus Átha Cliath: There are a number of bargain fares available, on a daily, weekly and monthly basis, which are excellent value, such as: Bus only, unlimited travel; Bus and Rail, unlimited travel. There are a number of shops and post office commuter ticket outlets. Such information, including a guide to Dublin Bus Services, is contained in the *Dublin Bus Timetable*. For details contact Dublin Bus, 59 Upper O'Connell Street, Dublin 1. Tel: (01) 873 4222. Web: www.dublinbus.ie

Bus Éireann: Tel: (01) 836 6111 for details concerning provincial bus and expressway services. Web: www.buseireann.ie

Iarnród Éireann/Irish Rail: Tel: (01) 836 6222. 24-hour talking timetable: 1890 778899. Website: www.irishrail.ie

Tourist Information Offices
Dublin Tourism Centre, Suffolk Street, Dublin 2. Tel: (01) 605 7700. Web: www.visitdublin.com

Galway City: Aras Failte, Forster Street, Galway. Tel: (091) 537 700. Web: www.irelandwest.ie

Cork City: Aras Failte, Grand Parade, Cork. Tel: (021) 425 5100.
Web: www.corkkerry.ie

If you require tourist information, or accommodation booked, contact the Tourist Office.

James Joyce Tower and Museum, Sandycove: Tel: (01) 280 9265.
Email: joycetower@dublintourism.ie

James Joyce Centre: 35 North Great George's Street, Dublin 1.
Tel: (01) 878 8547.
Email: info@jamesjoyce.ie
Web: www.jamesjoyce.ie

Irish Writers' Museum, 18 Parnell Square North, Dublin 1.
Tel: (01) 872 2077.
Web: www.writerscentre.ie

The Nora Barnacle House, 8 Bowling Green, Galway.
Tel: (091) 564 743.
Web: www.norabarnacle.com

Newman House, 85/86 St Stephen's Green, Dublin 2.
Tel: (01) 716 7422.

Select Bibliography

Bradley, Bruce, SJ, *James Joyce's Schooldays*, Gill & Macmillan 1982.

Budgen, Frank, *James Joyce and the making of Ulysses*, Grayson 1934.

Bulfin, William, *Rambles in Eirinn*, H. Gill & Son Ltd 1907.

Byrne, J.F., *Silent Years*, New York 1953.

Costello, Peter, *James Joyce – The Years of Growth 1882–1915*. Kyle Cathie Ltd 1992.

Craig, Maurice, *Dublin 1660–1860*, The Cresset Press 1952.

Curran, C.P., *James Joyce Remembered*, Oxford University Press 1968.

Ellmann, Richard, *James Joyce*, (revised edition) Oxford University Press 1982.

Gorman, Herbert, *James Joyce*, Bodley Head 1941.

Healy, George Harris ed., *The Dublin Diary of Stanislaus Joyce*, Faber and Faber 1962.

Hutchins, Patricia, *James Joyce's World*, Methuen 1957.

Joyce, James, *A Portrait of the Artist as a Young Man*, B.W. Huebsch 1916.

—*Dubliners: The Corrected Text*, Jonathan Cape 1967.*Letters of James Joyce, Vol.1* (ed. Stuart Gilbert), Faber and Faber 1957.

Letters of James Joyce, Vol. 11 and 111 (ed. Richard Ellmann), Faber and Faber 1966.

Selected Letters of James Joyce (ed. Richard Ellmann), The Viking Press 1975.

Joyce, Stanislaus, *My Brother's Keeper*, Faber & Faber 1958.

Joyce, Weston St John, *The Neighbourhood of Dublin*, 1912 (revised edition) Gill & Macmillan 1939.

Kain, Richard, *Dublin in the Age of William Butler Yeats and James Joyce*, University of Oklahoma Press 1967.

King, Carlyle, *Interview with Eileen Vance*, December 1953.

Maddox, Brenda, *Nora, A Biography of Nora Joyce*, Hamish Hamilton 1988; Minerva 1989.

O'Connor, Ulick, *The Joyce We Knew*, Mercier Press 1967.

O'Dwyer, Frederick, *Lost Dublin*, Gill & Macmillan 1985.

Power, Arthur, *Conversations with James Joyce*, Millington 1974. The Lilliput Press 1999.

Rose, Danis, "Soldier Than Most: John Joyce's House in North Richmond Street." *James Joyce Quarterly Vol 31, Number 2, Winter 1994.*

Sheehy, Eugene, *May it Please the Court*, C.J. Fallon Ltd 1951.

Stephenson, Paul and Margie Waters, " 'We Two' and the Lost Angel: The Cousins of Sandymount and James Joyce." *James Joyce Quarterly Vol. 37, Numbers 1 and 2, Fall 1999 and Winter 2000.*

Sullivan, Kevin, *Joyce among the Jesuits*, Columbia University Press 1958.

Thom's Official Directory of Dublin City and County, 1875–1912.

Further Reading

Hart, Clive and Ian Gunn with Harold Beck, *James Joyce's Dublin – A Topographical Guide to the Dublin of Ulysses*, Thames & Hudson 2004.

Killeen, Terence, *Ulysses Unbound – a reader's companion to James Joyce's Ulysses*, Wordwell/National Library of Ireland 2004.

Murphy, Niall, *A Bloomsday Postcard*, The Lilliput Press 2004.

Nicholson, Robert, *The Ulysses Guide – Tours through Joyce's Dublin*, New Island 2002.

Index